T0295550

# TOURISM AND HOSPITALITY MANAGEMENT IN PRACTICE

*Tourism and Hospitality Management in Practice: A Case Study Collection* is a collection of real-world business cases with a particular focus on small- and medium-sized enterprises (SMEs) in different countries from around the world. Fifteen compact cases capture a variety of business situations that present decisions, opportunities, or challenges. Organised into four parts, the cases reflect the various impacts of changing external conditions and internal factors in tourism and hospitality SMEs.

Each case tells the story of a particular business situation and context, and the student takes on the role of the decision maker. All cases include a synopsis, discussion questions, a learning activity, references, and suggested reading. An introductory chapter written specifically for students offers advice on what to expect from learning with a case, as well as hints on how to approach a case analysis. The cases offer multiple opportunities to connect tourism and hospitality knowledge and theory to practice, with a particular emphasis on analytical skill development, problem-solving, and alternative generation.

This case collection is suitable for undergraduate and graduate courses in tourism, hospitality management, and business, as well as for professional development programs.

For instructors who teach with the cases, there are teaching notes, comprising comprehensive teaching plans and resources, learning activities, reflective questions, additional readings, and external resources, all available online.

**Rebecca Wilson-Mah**, EdD, is an associate professor in the School of Tourism and Hospitality Management and program head for the MA in tourism management at Royal Roads University, Canada. An award-winning case writer and reviewer, Rebecca creates applied, accessible, and authentic learning experiences with a particular focus on teaching with cases.

## International Cases in Business and Management

Series Editors: Gina Vega and Rob Edwards

This series of textbooks has been developed to provide students and lecturers with high-quality, peer-reviewed, and concise teaching cases, which explore key business and management topics set in real-life scenarios around the world.

All cases included in each book are short – between 1500 and 2500 words – and are crafted to encourage class discussion and critical reflection. Cases are accompanied by a rich range of online resources for instructors, making effective and rewarding discussion in the classroom and corporate training room easy. All cases are real-world, with no composites and no invented situations. Some of them come from secondary sources, some from personal experience, and some from field research.

The series is suitable for all levels of university education, including MBA and Executive Education, and organisational training environments.

**Doing Business in South Asia**
*G. V. Muralidhara*

**Tourism and Hospitality Management in Practice: A Case Study Collection**
*Edited by Rebecca Wilson-Mah*

# TOURISM AND HOSPITALITY MANAGEMENT IN PRACTICE

## A Case Study Collection

*Edited by Rebecca Wilson-Mah*

Routledge
Taylor & Francis Group
LONDON AND NEW YORK

First published 2024
by Routledge
4 Park Square, Milton Park, Abingdon, Oxon OX14 4RN

and by Routledge
605 Third Avenue, New York, NY 10158

*Routledge is an imprint of the Taylor & Francis Group, an informa business*



*British Library Cataloguing-in-Publication Data*
A catalogue record for this book is available from the British Library

*Library of Congress Cataloguing-in-Publication Data*
Names: Wilson-Mah, Rebecca, editor.
Title: Tourism and hospitality management in practice : a case study collection / edited by Rebecca Wilson-Mah.
Description: New York : Routledge, 2024. | Series: International cases in business mangement; volume 2 | Includes bibliographical references and index.
Identifiers: LCCN 2023030237 (print) | LCCN 2023030238 (ebook) | ISBN 9781032247670 (hbk) | ISBN 9781032247601 (pbk) | ISBN 9781003280040 (ebk)
Subjects: LCSH: Tourism--Management--Case studies. | Hospitality industry--Management--Case studies. | Small business--Management--Case studies.
Classification: LCC G155.A1 T58934853 2024 (print) | LCC G155.A1 (ebook) | DDC 647.068--dc23/eng/20230901
LC record available at https://lccn.loc.gov/2023030237
LC ebook record available at https://lccn.loc.gov/2023030238

ISBN: 978-1-032-24767-0 (hbk)
ISBN: 978-1-032-24760-1 (pbk)
ISBN: 978-1-003-28004-0 (ebk)

DOI: 10.4324/9781003280040

Typeset in Galliard
by MPS Limited, Dehradun

Access the Support Material: www.routledge.com/9781032247601

# CONTENTS

# ACKNOWLEDGEMENTS

From the Volume Editor

This volume of Tourism and Hospitality Cases has been made possible through the contributions of 22 authors. The cases are typically collaborations between two or more co-authors. These collaborations have inspired the development of teaching cases that reflect diverse management problems and practices in a range of contexts. Some authors are academics, others are practitioners, many are both. Six authors are graduate students who collaborated with their professors to research and write a case. All the authors share a passion for writing real-world factual cases that bring this global and dynamic industry into the classroom.

# ABOUT THE EDITOR AND CONTRIBUTORS

## Volume Editor

**Rebecca Wilson-Mah** is an associate professor in the School of Tourism and Hospitality Management at Royal Roads University, British Columbia, Canada. An award-winning case writer and case reviewer, Rebecca enjoys teaching with cases, mentoring new case writers, and collaborating with co-authors.

## Contributors

**Jo Axe** is a professor and the founding director of the School of Education and Technology at Royal Roads University and the program head for the MA in interdisciplinary studies.

**Daniel Bernardes** holds an MA in tourism management and has hotel management experience in South America, Europe, and North America.

**Jill Bueddefeld** is a PhD graduate from the University of Manitoba and is a post-doctoral fellow in the Department of Environment and Geography, at Wilfrid Laurier University in Waterloo, Ontario, Canada.

**Gillian Dixon** With a 25-year career in the restaurant industry, Gillian Dixon has run internationally acclaimed restaurants in London and New York. Gillian holds an MA in tourism management and shares her knowledge and experience in undergraduate courses related to career development, events management, and ethics.

**Megan Douglas** is an associate professor and department chair at Missouri Southern State University's Plaster School of Business.

**Catherine Evans** Founder of adventure company Tours of Exploration, Catherine Evans links conscientious travellers to like-minded hosts in remote destinations on all seven continents. Catherine is an associate faculty member at Royal Roads University in the School of Tourism and Hospitality Management.

**Sarah Holtzen** is an assistant professor of management at Missouri Southern State University's Plaster School of Business.

**Nigel Jarvis** is tourism and events course leader and principal lecturer in the School of Business and Law, University of Brighton.

**Jonelle Knowles** is a faculty member in Tourism, Recreation and Hospitality at Vancouver Island University specialising in food and beverage management, special events, and marketing.

**Charles Krusekopf** is a professor in the Royal Roads University School of Business and program head of the MBA program. He is an academic entrepreneur with a focus on developing new academic programs and opportunities across a range of fields and locations around the globe.

**Khanh Le** holds an MA in tourism management and is Assistant Food & Beverage Manager at Oak Bay Beach Hotel. Her particular interest in food and beverage was inspired by the rich food culture in Vietnam, her home country.

**Gabriela Leiß** is based in Austria. She returned to management after 12 years in academia and is head of people development in a multinational production enterprise.

**Katherine MacRae** is the executive director of the Commercial Bear Viewing Association of British Columbia, where she advocates for wild bears and their ecosystems and the bear viewing industry. Katherine is an associate faculty member in the School of Tourism and Hospitality Management at Royal Roads University, British Columbia, Canada.

**Giovanni Malcolm** is a project manager leading a team responsible for bringing battery electric bus technology to British Columbia, Canada. Giovani holds an MA in tourism management.

**Oluwafisayo Olayinka-Bello** is an award-winning travel blogger with an MA in tourism management.

**Sandra Cherro Osorio** is head of Program for the Bachelor of Business and Hospitality Management at Melbourne Polytechnic, Australia.

**Szilvia Paradi** specialises in tourism marketing, where she hones her skills working as a marketing specialist for a travel agency and a regional destination marketing organisation. Szilvia holds an MA in tourism management.

**Himal Poudel** has long been engaged in various rural and community-based tourism activities in Nepal and holds an MA in tourism management.

**Esha Thukral** is a lecturer in business at Melbourne Polytechnic, Melbourne, Australia.

**Christine Van Winkle** is a professor in the Faculty of Kinesiology and Recreation Management at the University of Manitoba, where she teaches tourism and event management.

**Brian White** is a professor in the School of Tourism and Hospitality at Royal Roads University.

**Anita Zehrer** is a professor and head of the Family Business Center as well as head of Research at the MCI Management Center Innsbruck, Austria.

# INTRODUCTION

Welcome to the International Cases in Business Management series and this special case volume of *Tourism and Hospitality Management in Practice.*

This volume brings together a focus on small- and medium-sized tourism and hospitality enterprises (SMEs) in different countries, with cases from Australia, Austria, Canada, Nepal, the United Kingdom, the United States, and Vietnam. Some of the cases re-visit the resilience and creativity in SMEs during a lengthy period of pandemic uncertainty and recovery. The cases capture a variety of managerial decisions that organisations have taken to survive and thrive, re-focus their client relationships, adapt their business models, or to shift their operating systems and resources. Tourism studies are interdisciplinary, as such, these cases connect to pressing societal concerns such as sustainability, climate change, and resilience.

The cases offer multiple opportunities to connect knowledge to practise with a particular emphasis on decision making, analytical skill development, and problem-solving processes.

The cases are suitable for undergraduate and graduate courses in tourism and hospitality management and general business.

If you are an instructor, you can request an accompanying teaching note for each case online at http://www.routledge.com/9781032247601.

The cases in this volume are developed from primary research with managers and leaders in small- and medium-sized enterprises in the tourism and hospitality sector. The cases all relate to significant strategic or managerial decisions in tourism and hospitality SMEs and are organised into four themed parts.

**Part 1: Resilience and Recovery**
**Part 2: Sustainable Tourism in Context**
**Part 3: Operations Management**
**Part 4: Events and the Visitor Experience**

DOI: 10.4324/9781003280040-1

## Cases by Part: An Overview

### *Part 1: Resilience and Recovery*

The cases in Part 1 reflect the diversity in the tourism and hospitality industry and the resilience of SMEs. The cases reflect 1) the onset of the pandemic, 2) during the pandemic, or, 3) during the recovery phase. The COVID-19 related cases offer a "window" on what was happening in some SMEs. This was a period of unprecedented uncertainty and disruption that has transformed the sector in all respects.

**Case 1,** "Pivoting in the Tourism Sector: COVID-19," showcases the challenges faced by the small ship cruise sector that operated multi-day excursions of British Columbia, Canada's spectacular west coast.

Maple Leaf Adventures offered small ship cruises and multi-day excursions in Canada's spectacular coastal locations on the west coast of British Columbia. Kevin Smith, the owner of Maple Leaf Adventures had a pressing need to identify the content and process of possible pivots for the SMEs operating in the area.

#### Learning Objectives

1 Explain the concept of a business pivot.
2 Identify the COVID-19 related business impacts on SMEs.
3 Identify business pivot options for SMEs through collective thinking.
4 Create a plan to bring small businesses together to solve problems with a focus on identifying who should be at the table and why.

**Case 2,** "A Case of Resilience and Agility: The Craigdarroch Castle," highlights how a non-profit heritage museum needed a process to plan for a COVID-19 closure.

Craigdarroch Castle, a non-profit tourist attraction and a national historic site, operated solely on memberships, donations, special events, and admission fees. In March 2020, as COVID-19 became a public health emergency, John Hughes, Executive Director, announced that Craigdarroch Castle was closed until further notice. Hughes needed a process and framework that would help him, and the team, adapt to the operating restrictions and all the operational changes needed to respond to COVID-19.

#### Learning Objectives

1 Develop a process and a framework that an organisation could use to adapt to the operating restrictions in disasters or emergencies.
2 Explore planning tools for problems that have tight time constraints and unpredictable external variables.
3 Identify opportunities to keep employees working that align with operational needs during pandemic restrictions.

**Case 3,** "A Sudden Inhospitable Situation: The Everglade Hotel," is a race to bring a leadership team together to quickly formulate an emergency plan and contingency plan for the hotel.

The Everglade Hotel had just completed a lengthy period of renovations to the public areas, including the lobby and the restaurant. Anticipation was high for a busy summer season, and the occupancy rate was forecast to be around 77%. When COVID-19 became a public health issue, the Hotel had to shift gears quickly. Kim Douglas, Director of Rooms, was tasked with bringing the hotel leadership together to develop a joint emergency plan and contingency plan.

### Learning Objectives

1 Produce an emergency response for a hotel closing process that covers all aspects of the operation and the needs of the business, guests, and employees.
2 Write a Gantt chart or similar for the emergency response actions proposed for the Rooms Division.
3 Integrate the values of the organisation with the actions proposed.
4 Develop a contingency plan for the Rooms Division

**Case 4,** "Tourism Resort Employers and Employees Adapt to Pandemic Uncertainty," shares employer and employee experiences in Whistler, a mountain resort in British Columbia, Canada.

In April 2020 two researchers Sam Brown and Rachel Lee decided they would support tourism employees and employers in the early days of the pandemic by studying how employers and employees were experiencing their workplace environments. This case offers students an opportunity to identify appropriate employer responses to address the unique characteristics of an uncertain external emergency with prolonged impact.

### Learning Objectives

1 Identify the impacts of lengthy periods of uncertainty on employees.
2 Develop appropriate responses to address the unique characteristics of an uncertain event or circumstances.
3 Identify limitations in a data set.
4 Make recommendations for the implementation of specific employer practises in periods of uncertainty that also support business recovery.

### *Part 2: Sustainable Tourism in Context*

The cases focus on a range of approaches taken to contribute to a sustainable path for tourism development and operations in different contexts.

**Case 5,** "Rural Tourism Growth in Ghalegaun, Nepal," introduces a tourism leader Prem Bahadur Ghale, and his work to support sustainable tourism development within a small village in Western Nepal.

In 2018, Ghalegaun, a small village in western Nepal faced tourism growth challenges. The homestay village had generated gradual growth in tourism, yet in 2018 the chairperson of the local Tourism Management Committee (TMC), Prem Bahadur Ghale was concerned about meeting the demand for homestays. The village had to consider what was suitable for rural tourism growth for Ghalegaun and develop a shared community approach.

### Learning Objectives

1 Identify the issues, challenges, risks, and opportunities associated with sustainable rural tourism development in a specific rural community.
2 Evaluate the long-term viability of rural tourism development by applying a nine-stage plan to effectively sustain community-based tourism (CBT) in a developing tourism destination.

**Case 6,** "Sustainable Tourism Plan and Rebrand for Lagos, Nigeria," explores the push pull theory of travel motivation with a focus on Lagos, Nigeria.

Adun Okupe, CEO of Red Clay Advisory, and her team were appointed to develop and translate the Lagos State Tourism Master Plan (LSTMP) into a simplified tourism plan. The major constraints for Red Clay Advisory for the project were the six-week timeline and tourism stakeholders' lack of proper understanding of the tourism plan. The international media had emphasised Nigeria's shortcomings, and this had tarnished the country's reputation as an unsafe place for tourists and investors.

### Learning Objectives

1 Identify how different motivations to travel are met or not met in a particular destination.
2 Develop the action steps for a travel consulting project based on available information and the needs of the client.
3 Identify opportunities to re-brand a specific destination and explain how the rebrand could contribute to economic sustainability.

**Case 7,** "Local I'a: A Social Enterprise Makes a Big Impact on a Small Scale," examines Local I'a, a social enterprise in Hawaii that operated as a sustainable fresh seafood retailer.

Local I'a sourced seafood and products from local fishers, with a model of purchasing seasonal local seafood at a fair market value directly from the fishers and selling direct to restaurant and individual consumers. At the heart of sustainable "pono" fishing practises was emphasising the importance of respecting the environment and maintaining a balance between human activities and nature. While the concept was admired by sustainable food advocates and the media, Ashley Watts, owner of Local I'a, believed more impact could be made, especially with the restaurant industry sector.

### Learning Objectives

1 Apply concepts related to the four pillars of sustainability: economic, environmental, social, and cultural.
2 Explain the concept of a social enterprise.
3 Rationalise the resources required to expand existing business opportunities in a sustainable enterprise.
4 Explain the pros and cons of including sustainably sourced items on a restaurant menu.

### *Part 3: Operations Management*

Bringing international cases from Australia, Austria, Canada, the USA, and Vietnam, these cases profile a range of operational issues faced by small business owners.

**Case 8,** "The Peak Hotel: The Challenge of Succession and Family Firm Continuity," takes the reader inside a hotel business in Lermoos, Austria, that is working to develop a family succession plan. A family-run four-star hotel in the Austrian Alps has challenges with family firm succession. The family firm is currently in its second generation, and the owners, Perry and Patricia, want to develop a plan to hand the business to the next generation. The entrepreneurial family is dealing with change and transformation processes among the family members.

#### Learning Objectives

1 Identify the strengths and interests of each of the family members.
2 List and discuss the issues related to intra-family succession at the Peak Hotel.
3 Develop strategies for the family to consider for working together effectively.
4 Identify the pros and cons of different strategies of business succession.
5 Suggest other options the family could pursue for the business beside family succession.

**Case 9,** "Marketing Strategy for Business Recovery: Tours of Exploration, a Travel Agency," is a case that propels the reader inside a travel agency and the conversations that occurred as the business planned during an uncertain time.

Until early 2020, Catherine Evans founder and owner of Tours of Exploration had a successful tour business with both international and domestic clients. Things changed abruptly in March 2020, when the pandemic threw chaos on Evans' business. Caught in a no revenue financial situation, with expenses and a heavy workload, and uncertainty ahead, Evans was tasked with determining how to adjust her digital marketing strategy to a recovery pandemic marketing plan for Tours of Exploration. With several alternatives to consider, she had to make a strategic choice.

#### Learning Objectives

1 Identify factors that contribute to how a small business over time builds a marketing strategy.
2 Within the parameters of a specific budget, explore, prioritise, and recommend a marketing strategy for business recovery and related tactics from a range of options.

**Case 10,** "Here's a Tip: Paying It Forward May Backfire at Oven and Tap," explores tip sharing practises in a restaurant in Arkansas, USA, and the unexpected repercussions of a large gratuity.

One evening in December Grant Wise, a local real estate marketing entrepreneur dining with 40 business professionals, announced, "We are tipping a total of four thousand, four hundred dollars!" This case captures the disagreements and decisions that ensued. The case explores inter-related aspects of compensation, equity theory, tipping policy, and procedures and tip sharing practise in the food and beverage industry in the USA.

### Learning Objectives

1 Evaluate the fairness of tip sharing using equity theory.
2 Analyse responses employees may have to perceived inequity in the workplace using equity theory as a basis for analysis.
3 Write an ethical tip-sharing policy and procedure that balances competing concerns for pay equity.

**Case 11,** "Street Food in Ho Chi Minh City: Managing High Demand," is a case situated in Ho Chi Minh City with a new business that has decisions to make to balance food production, delivery, and demand.

Thien Tran opened Shaanxi Bao, a street food restaurant offering take-out-only buns in Ho Chi Minh City, Vietnam. Two weeks after opening, there was a constant line-up in front of the restaurant for both online and direct food orders. Each customer had to wait for at least 25–30 minutes before reaching the front of the line. The goal in the opening plan for a unique customer service experience was not fully delivered, and Tran was concerned.

### Learning Objectives

1 Identify some operational adjustments that are often needed to support a new restaurant business.
2 Redesign a food distribution strategy to improve the customer experience.

**Case 12,** "A Story of Resilience at the Restaurant Comida Corrida," explores Frank Camorra, who proudly opened Tres a Cinco at Hosier Lane in Melbourne's central business district. Camorra had appointed Chef Sarai Castillo as Head Chef, and Castillo had retained the staff that had worked with her during the pandemic. This was a success story for Camorra and Castillo, one that told the story of resilience, and it was a story they both wanted to share with other businesses and employees.

### Learning Objectives

1 Explain the impact of COVID-19 on restaurant employees and restaurant businesses.
2 Analyse the linkages between individual resilience and organisational resilience.
3 Evaluate the importance of optimising business operations and leveraging new strategies and solutions to manage a crisis.

### *Part 4: Events and the Visitor Experience*

The cases in this part share the possibilities events and visitor experiences present to attract visitation, entertain, and contribute to the local economy. Events also educate, inform, and transform beyond the initial visit, offering the possibility of influencing post-visit behaviour.

**Case 13,** "Game, Set, and Match: Increasing the Economic Impact of a Tennis Tournament in Eastbourne, England," explores the multiplier effect and the strategies that encourage visitors to extend their stay.

The Eastbourne Borough Council helped manage an annual major tennis tournament. The Council was looking for advice and suggestions to make their day tripper tennis fans stay longer and ultimately spend more money in Eastbourne. This would help to create a stronger tourism multiplier effect for Eastbourne. Any strategies should also help to inspire visitor satisfaction so that visitors would return to the destination in future years. How might the Council encourage visitors to stay longer to make their day tripper tennis fans stay longer and ultimately spend more money?

### Learning Objectives

1 Understand and explain the significance of the tourism multiplier for a local economy.
2 Suggest the essential elements of a positive sport tourism event experience.
3 Design an event program strategy to maximise the length of stay and spend of day trippers.
4 Identify the potential limitations at events when seeking to extend stay and increase spend.

**Case 14,** "From Visitors to Trusted Messengers: Encouraging Climate Change Action through Post-visit Action Resources," explores how, after an on-site experience, attractions can connect with visitors beyond the initial visit.

The Assiniboine Park Zoo (APZ), operated by the not-for-profit Assiniboine Park Conservancy, had a strong conservation and research mandate that focused on arctic and subarctic species. This case explores how, after an on-site experience, attractions can connect with visitors beyond the initial visit, to build lasting relationships and develop "trusted messengers" who may later contribute to the organisation's mandate and conservation action.

### Learning Objectives

1 Identify how on-site experiences can be used to connect with visitors beyond the initial visit and build lasting relationships to contribute to the organisation's mission.
2 Identify specific ways that an organisation can develop visitors into trusted messengers who support climate action awareness and related behaviour post-visit.

**Case 15,** "The Local Wild Food Challenge: Translating a Chef's Passion for Wild Food into a Sustainable Event," is the story of a Chef who had a goal to celebrate community, and, at the same time, generate awareness of natural resources and the local environment.

Chef Bill Manson created a small community event, the "Local Wild Food Challenge," in 2008 in Eastbourne, New Zealand. In 2018 the event had become a network of communities holding yearly events in different countries celebrating the culinary skills of local people. With expansion Manson recognised that he needed to give more consideration to community event planning and organisation while also staying true to his commitment to inclusivity and promoting sustainability of local resources.

### Learning Objectives

1 Identify and explain the essential elements of an event experience with a particular focus on co-creation and inclusivity.

2 Apply the event management body of knowledge (EMBOK) to an event in order to identify and list strengths and potential gaps.
3 Design a sustainable event program plan for an event going through the full design process.
4 Create a visual mind map or description of the outcomes (cognitive, emotional, behavioural) that can occur at an event.

# CASE PREPARATION AND ANALYSIS FOR STUDENTS[1]

*Gina Vega and Rob Edwards*

"It is not that I'm so smart. But I stay with the questions much longer."
~Albert Einstein

## Why Are You in This Class?

Perhaps you are focusing your studies on challenges specific to hospitality and tourism. Perhaps you are taking this class as an elective. Maybe you are a business major who wants to learn a bit more about the issues that companies in hospitality and tourism globally are facing. Maybe this class was the only one open that fit into your schedule.

None of that matters. What does matter is your willingness to participate in your own learning, rather than wait for someone to *tell* you what to learn.

## What to Expect from a Case-Based Class

If you are used to a traditional lecture format class, a case class will be a big change for you.

In a traditional class, you are the recipient of knowledge. The instructor is the giver of knowledge, and you receive her words of wisdom passively.

In a case class, you are the creator of knowledge and the discoverer of insights. The instructor is your guide and your facilitator, and she shares in the creation and discovery processes with you.

In a traditional class, the instructor works hard, and you sit quietly. You can send in a tape recorder and listen to the lecture later. You can watch a video and play computer games. You can check your email. You can update your Facebook account.

In a case class, you both work hard and are very much present. You are alert the whole time, because you are responsible for your learning and the learning processes of your classmates. Case learning is social learning and requires active involvement.

DOI: 10.4324/9781003280040-2

Here's how it works:

- You read the assigned case ahead of class. You might consider trying the Three Reads Model in Appendix 1.
  - Take notes as to the individuals involved, the situations presented, and any connections you can make to theory or analogous characters or situations you have been exposed to before, either in classes or in your work or life experience.
  - Identify your assumptions and the information that is missing for you to do a thorough analysis.
  - List the problems and select one problem to focus on at a time. Most cases present multiple problems; your ability to identify a key problem will give your case analysis structure and meaning.
  - Do any preliminary analysis you can, such as financial comparisons and ratios, statistical analyses or other quantitative explorations. If your analysis is to be qualitative, determine the foundation of your analysis and articulate reasons for and against a strategy or position.
  - Write down as many possible recommendations as you can, then select one and commit to it.
- Go to class and get ready for an engaged discussion.
  - The instructor may start off with a précis of the case (or ask you to provide one) and then toss out some icebreaker questions – easy questions to get the conversation moving.
  - The instructor may continue to toss questions to the group or, depending on personal style, may ask questions or opinions directly of one individual.
  - The instructor will tease out a series of analyses, decision-making perspectives, and positions from the class members
  - The class reaches a conclusion, recommendation, decision, or final analysis.
- You may be assigned to a team.
  - If you have been assigned to a case team before the classroom discussion, your preparation should take place with this team.
  - You can expect a lot of lively discussion during the preparation phase, and you will generally (but not always) come to agreement before class.
  - The class discussion will be between team positions rather than individual positions and will proceed as above.

**Hints for success in a case class:**

- Be prepared.
- Participate actively.
- Allow your emotions to become involved along with your critical analysis.
- Respect your peers' input.
- Try to understand the alternative perspectives put forth in the classroom.
- If on a team, be a "good" team member – no one likes a free rider.

## Two Different Types of Cases

There are two different types of cases: decision-based cases and descriptive or illustrative cases.

**TABLE 0.1** Types of Cases

| | *Decision-Based Cases* | *Descriptive or Illustrative Cases* |
|---|---|---|
| Description | Decision-based cases will require you to make a reasoned recommendation, supported by facts and theory, for the case protagonist to follow. | Descriptive or illustrative cases do not conclude with a call for a recommendation. Instead, they present a situation that has occurred, and your job is to analyse the protagonist's actions. |
| Example | Your recommendation might be for the protagonist to seek alternative sources of funding rather than depending on friends and family. Some sources he might consider include a bank line of credit, loans, or angel investors. These three sources involve less emotional investment and more straightforward financial analysis to convince lenders. | You may determine that she should have taken a different set of action steps that might have led to a better outcome. Or you may decide that the actions taken were justified and provided the best outcomes under the existing circumstances. Or, your recommendation might be to take advantage of a favourable economy to expand now rather than waiting until the company has accumulated more assets. Even though the protagonist tends to be conservative in his approach to expansion, it makes sense to exploit opportunities that present themselves. It may be a less secure position to take, but the potential rewards may be greater. |

In either type of case, your job will be clear to you, if not from the narrative, then from the questions that follow the case. Be sure to read and think about those questions and use them as guidance in your analysis.

### Preparing a Written Case Analysis

The cases in this book are short, designed specifically to help you focus on the key aspects of problems presented. You will, of course, find information in the cases that is not directly relevant to the main problem. Pay attention to this information, as it is likely to be important in your analysis. However, it will not drive your analysis, which should be focused, instead, on the topical components presented in each case.

The analysis of a full-length case can be expected to take a significant amount of time to complete. The analysis of a short case should be, by its nature, short. It will contain all (or most) of the elements described below, but the elements will be short and concise. It is likely that your analysis will include answers to (or take direction from) the questions at the end of the case.

Although it may sound easy to write a short case analysis, do not allow yourself to be tricked into thinking that such an analysis is a snap to put together. It requires discipline to write concisely and to explain complex concepts using simple, clear language. That will be your challenge throughout this course. The examples included in this chapter are based on finance; your cases will likely have a different focus.

## Written Analysis of a Short Decision-Based Finance Case

If you are preparing for a class discussion, the Three Reads Method (Appendix 1) will suffice. However, if you have been assigned a **written analysis of a decision-based case,** it can be hard to know where to start. The following model can help you complete a clear and organised decision-based analysis. You can generally use tables, formulas, or matrices instead of narrative sentences if they will support your analysis better.

1 *Executive Summary*
Write this section last even though it appears first in the case analysis. The goal of the executive summary is to provide a **brief** overview of the main issues, the proposed recommendation, and the actions to follow (2 or 3 sentences).
2 *Statement of the Problem*
Describe the core problem(s) of the case and the decision(s) to be made by the protagonist. Include the symptoms of the problem(s) and differentiate them from the problem(s) themselves. For example, the spots on your face are a symptom. The problem is that you have the measles (or acne, or an allergy to some skin product, or some other infection). This statement of the problem is a **diagnostic process**, and you need to build the rationale for your diagnosis into this section (2 or 3 sentences).
3 *Causes*
This section is an exploration and discussion of potential causes of the main case problem(s). Support your exploration by the application of relevant theories from this course or others. Be sure to use analytical tools that will support your decision-making process and will illustrate your analysis (2 or 3 sentences).
4 *Possible Solutions/Alternatives*
Surface as many possible solutions or alternative actions as you can. You should not limit your possibilities to what you think is easy to accomplish or logical, but rather entertain a wide variety of options. You do not have to recommend all of these options, but you need to make your instructor aware that you have considered them (2 or 3 sentences).
5 *Selection of Criteria and Analysis of Alternatives*
Select the criteria for determining the basic feasibility of the alternatives identified above. These criteria will guide you in considering the pros and cons of each feasible alternative. Consider at least three alternatives in this section. Sometimes, a tabular format will keep this section organised and clear. You should be prepared to provide analyses in this section (2 or 3 sentences or small matrix).
6 *Recommendation*
What do you recommend that the protagonist do? Support your recommendation with a rationale that is based both in facts and in the appropriate theory for the problem (*i.e.,* market analysis, financial statements analysis, the impact of organisational structure, supply chain management, or other disciplinary focus) (2 or 3 sentences).
7 *Implementation*
Your instructor may state that no case analysis is complete without providing the action steps to implement the recommendation. What steps should the protagonist take in order

to make your recommendation happen? Identify to the greatest extent possible the responsibilities, costs, timeline, and measurement of success of the final implementation.

Appendix 2 provides a sample written analysis of a short decision case.

### Written Analysis of a Short Descriptive or Illustrative Case

If you are preparing for a class discussion, the method mentioned above or the Three Reads Method at the end of the chapter will suffice. However, if you have been assigned a **written analysis of a descriptive or illustrative tourism case**, it can be hard to know where to start. The following model can help you complete a clear and organised analysis. You can generally use tables, formulas, or matrices instead of narrative sentences if they will support your analysis better.

1 *Executive summary*
  Write this section last even though it appears first in the case analysis. The goal of the executive summary is to provide a **brief** overview of the main issues, your analysis, and your conclusions (2 or 3 sentences).
2 *The facts*
  This is not simply a list of case facts. You need to determine which facts are relevant and which are simply background information or environmental "noise". If you are analysing a business ethics case, for example, it probably does not matter that the action takes place in the fall. However, in a tourism case it may well matter that the action occurs at the end of a busy season, a fiscal year, or at some other critical period.
  Draw facts not only from the case narrative but, notably, from the exhibits, attachments, financial records, spreadsheets, and other sources within the case. Be sure to peruse these figures carefully for possible errors, misinterpretations, and potential clues to case solutions. (bulleted list)
3 *Inferences to be drawn*
  Why did things happen as they did? What else might happen as a consequence? What are the implications of these actions in terms of attitudes and relationships? Financial decisions, especially in entrepreneurial environments, are rarely based solely on the numbers. Numbers are generally rational; people rarely are, and their decisions reflect this (2 or 3 sentences).
4 *Theory- and technique-based discussion of the case action*
  Apply relevant theory and financial analysis techniques to an explanation of actions and consequences, implications of actions and consequences, and the impact of various outcome criteria on the decisions that were made in the case. The true value of learning entrepreneurial finance lies in the use of actual data to guide future decisions and to draw sensible conclusions about potential outcomes. The financial analyses help you look to the future as well as reflect on the past (2 or 3 sentences).
5 *Options to the actions within the case*
  Compare the actions of the protagonist with the other courses of action that were open at the time. What might have been the logical outcomes of those actions? Determine a hierarchy of preferred actions based on outcome criteria you established in Part 4. This section may logically take a tabular format.

6 *Conclusion/Reflection*
   This is your rationale for preferred action. If the protagonist has done the right thing according to your analysis, explain why. If the protagonist should have done something else, explain why. Reflect on your reasoning. In a descriptive or illustrative case, your reflection is often the most valuable section because it is from these reflections that future courses of action will derive (2 or 3 sentences).

Appendix 3 provides a sample written analysis of a short descriptive case.

## How Will Your Written Case Analysis Be Evaluated?

Because case evaluation can be highly subjective, many instructors will prepare a rubric for you to measure your own work against. You can find a basic rubric that outlines generic instructor's expectations and clarifies the standard you should be aiming for in Appendix 4. Each instructor's rubric is unique, but the generic rubric provides some guidelines for you to follow.

Appendix 5 is a self-grading rubric to help you check your own work for completeness before submission. This self-grader will help to keep you "honest."

## List of Appendices

1 Preparing for a case discussion – The three reads model for a short case
2 Sample written case analysis for a short decision-based finance case
3 Sample written case analysis for a short descriptive/illustrative finance case
4 Generic grading rubric
5 Self-grading rubric

## Note

1 Adapted from: *Entrepreneurial Finance: Concepts and Cases, Second Edition* by Miranda S. Lam and Gina Vega, Copyright (2021) by Routledge Taylor & Francis. Reproduced by permission of Taylor & Francis Group.

## APPENDIX 1

### Preparing for a Case Discussion – The Three Reads Model for a Short Case

Reading and preparing a case for class discussion involves more than reading a blog, your email, a novel, or a chapter in a textbook. You can develop your case reading skills through the technique outlined below. This technique allows you to make the best possible contribution during the class case discussion. It requires you to read the case (even short cases) three times, twice briefly and once extensively. If you are working with a team, you will want to adapt this process to assure topical coverage.

#### *First Read*

- Find six minutes (yes, six minutes is enough for the one-to-four-page cases in this book) to sit down uninterrupted. Mute your phone so that you do not get distracted during this short reading period.
- Read the hook. This may be several paragraphs long in a full-length case, but just one or two sentences in the cases in this book. The hook will introduce you to the case "problem." Jot down the problem in the margin.
- Read the first sentence (and only the first sentence) of each paragraph in the case. Write a keyword or two in the margin next to the paragraph.
- Read the titles only of any attachments and exhibits.
- Turn your phone back on and go about your business.

#### *Second Read*

- This is the big one – a two-page case will take you at least 30 minutes. Remember that if you have interruptions, this period must be extended.
- Read the entire case, slowly and carefully. Jot notes as you go along about the characters and their behaviour, the situation, and the action. Sometimes preparing a timeline of action makes it easier to follow and remember. Be sure to include any exhibits and attachments during this read.
- Jot down your own response to the situation and the characters, even if it's unsupported by theories or formal concepts. Make any connections you can to analogous situations you have experienced or read about. What are the differences or similarities to this situation? Remember, these notes that you are making are yours alone – no one else will be looking at them. It doesn't matter if they are messy, have lines drawn all over them, are put together in right-brain or left-brain style, just as long as they exist. They are meant to help you.
- Make a list of the assumptions you are making, the financial analyses you need to conduct, and the information you still need before you make a recommendation. Something is always missing, or the case would be really boring. So, what is missing?
- List the alternative solutions to the case, their pros and cons, and then select one recommendation. You always have to commit to one recommendation and provide a rationale for it. This recommendation should be supported by theory, experience, quantitative analysis, or other rationale.

- Prepare any case questions you have been assigned. Be sure to check any spreadsheets for errors or misinterpretations.
- You should be tired at this point. Put the case away.

*Third Read*

- This last read takes place not too long before class. The point of it is to make sure that the case is fresh in your mind and that you are still comfortable with your recommendation.
- This read resembles the first read: read the beginning, the first sentence of each paragraph, etc. But this time, include both your marginal notes and the notes you have made during the second read. You will need these notes to participate actively in class. Remember that class participation means that you have to talk – it's OK to read aloud what you have written if you are uncomfortable talking off the cuff.
- The entire process has taken two hours or less, which is about two thirds the amount of time you should anticipate using for class preparation for a 1½ hour class. If your class period is longer than this, your preparation should be commensurately more extensive.

## APPENDIX 2

### Sample Written Case Analysis for a Short Decision-Based Finance Case[2]

*Executive Summary*

Koehler Propane was a small, family-owned propane dealer with a very small heating oil division inherited through a prior acquisition. A local heating oil dealer was put up for sale, and Koehler had to decide whether or not to purchase it, and if so, at what price and on what terms. The best strategy for Koehler is to offer a cash price of between $800,000 and 850,000.

*Statement of the Problem*

The propane and heating oil dealer industry was in the declining phase of its life cycle and was characterised by high fluctuations in revenue due to uncertainty in energy prices and weather, high fixed-assets requirement and regulations by both federal and state agencies. Competition was high and business growth either involved intense price competition or acquisition of competing companies. Koehler and his son had to decide whether to buy the heating oil company or to close down their own small heating oil division altogether.

*Causes*

Some of Koehler's current equipment needed replacement if he were to remain in the heating oil business. Koehler had an advantage over competing bidders in a cash deal but not in a stock deal. The four valuation methods (discounted cash flow valuation and multiples valuation, multiples valuation, EBITDA multiple method, and percent of annual sales + inventory method) range from $624,019 to $918,606, averaging $818,469. A reasonable cash price ranged from $800,000 to $850,000.

*Possible Solutions/Alternatives*

Koehler Propane had three alternatives:

- *Close down the oil business:* Closing down the heating oil business would eliminate a break-even/money-losing division and allow Koehler to stay focused on its core business of propane delivery, but it would be contrary to their vision of developing Koehler into a large energy company.
- *Purchase two new trucks to replace existing ones:* Purchasing new trucks requires capital investments into a potentially money-losing division. Given the low volume and the surcharge they had to pay due to lack of bulk storage, they were at a cost disadvantage, severely limiting their ability to compete on price.
- *Acquire the heating oil company:* This would advance Koehler toward a more diverse product line and increase the size of its business. It would provide Koehler bulk storage facilities and make them a major heating oil distributor in the vicinity. If Koehler failed to acquire the heating oil company, one of its competitors would gain entrance into its primary territory and Koehler would face increased competition in its propane business.

### *Selection of Criteria and Analysis of Alternatives*

Note that the assignment of values for the three alternatives is arbitrary and meant as an example only. You would assign values as relevant for your own analysis.

**TABLE 0.2** Selection of Criteria and Analysis of Alternatives

| *Criterion* | *Assigned Value* | *Pro* | *Con* |
|---|---|---|---|
| Growth | 40 | They want to be industry leaders, larger customer base | Declining industry, high competition |
| Diversification | 30 | One of the main business goals | High risk, expensive |
| Capital investment | 30 | More dependable equipment | Potential dedication of needed cash to non-liquid assets |

### *Recommendation*

Closing down the oil business is bad for growth, for diversification, and for capital investment. If quantified, the option has 0 value. Purchasing two new trucks is good for capital investment, but "iffy" for both growth and diversification. If quantified, the option has a potential value of 30+. Acquiring the heating oil company is good for growth, diversification, and capital investment. Quantified, the option has a potential value of 100.

Both companies are located in the same town, and the two owners have past business relationships; therefore, Koehler will have better knowledge of the oil company than competing bidders. Competing bidders may be unwilling to offer a cash deal, or they will likely offer a much lower cash price. Koehler has an advantage over competing bidders in a cash deal but not in a stock deal. Given the advantages of a cash deal to the oil company, the best strategy for Koehler is to offer a cash price.

### *Implementation*

1 Agree on a valuation
2 Structure the deal internally
3 Negotiate with the seller for a mutually agreeable acquisition

## Note

2 This abbreviated analysis was prepared from *The Offer Price* (Lam, M. & Luther, R. 2012, The CASE Journal, Vol 8.2).

## APPENDIX 3

### Sample Written Case Analysis for a Short Descriptive/Illustrative Finance Case[3]

1 **Executive summary**
A schoolteacher has decided to open a taqueria in a small, historic New England city. The problem is whether he should launch his business at the time of the case in light of the many challenges facing him. He could not provide all the necessary information and was reluctant to listen to advice. He should not launch his business at this time.

2 **The facts**
The entrepreneur knew a little bit about a lot of things, but not enough about any one of the functional elements of his business to run it on his own. He had insufficient funds to last through a dry spell; he was being pushed to launch because the landlord of his desired location was in a hurry to get the lease signed. He did not have a full liquor license. Money was tight, loans were nonexistent, and his debt to asset ratio did not approach the industry standard. It also looks like he needs to do a closer examination of his anticipated revenues.

3 **Inferences to be drawn**
The Howling Wolf is likely to create value for the customer, as there appears to be growing demand for this type of cuisine and there is little direct competition. However, the money-making potential of the restaurant is unclear, and the owner's ability to sustain operations with the proposed staff of family/friends is doubtful. A launch would be a high risk/minimal reward strategy.

4 **Theory- and technique-based discussion of the case action**
A SWOT analysis showed that he had some significant strengths and opportunities in terms of personal contacts and an opening in the restaurant market. His passion, product and service differentiation, and personal skills suggest that he can provide an appealing venue for locals to enjoy a unique culinary experience. Potential funders have not been found, the economy is weak (although beginning to rebound slightly), and money is scarce. Although the entrepreneur believes strongly in his restaurant, he has been unable to provide financials that support that belief for banks or other funders. Computing breakeven revenue and cash burn rate show that breakeven weekly revenue is 4.35% below the original estimate. Total monthly cash outflow excluding COGS is over $34k compared to a beginning cash balance of only $61k. If revenue is more than 23% below the original estimate, he will run out of cash in 6 months.

5 **Options to the actions within the case**
Decision criteria: Potential to make a good return. Likelihood of staying in business without a liquor license. Potential to survive on limited investment. Likelihood of family and friends to continue providing low-cost assistance.
The entrepreneur has to weigh the importance of each of the decision criteria before making his decision. There are two possible decisions that the entrepreneur could make:

- The entrepreneur could open based on the support that he had from his family and his experience with this type of cuisine and confidence that the tourist season would likely be able to cover the slow season.
- The entrepreneur could postpone opening until acquiring more funds, a liquor license, and business advisers.

## 6 Conclusion/Reflection

Based on the analyses above, I would not recommend launching the business at this time. I think the entrepreneur should find an angel or other investor to provide the financial stability that will cover him through the tough times during the first year of operations. He should continue his efforts to obtain a full liquor license. He should plan to invest in advertising prior to his launch, and he should conduct a full-scale location analysis prior to signing his lease.

## Note

3 This abbreviated analysis was prepared from the *Howling Wolf Taqueria: Feeding the Good Wolf* (Vega, G. & Lam, M., 2013, Case Research Journal, Vol 34, Issue 2).

## APPENDIX 4 GENERIC GRADING RUBRIC

### How Will My Written Case Analysis Be Evaluated?

Because evaluation can be highly subjective, many instructors will prepare a rubric for you to measure your own work against. This rubric outlines the instructor's expectations and clarifies the standard you should be aiming for. Each instructor's rubric is unique, but the generic rubric that follows provides some guidelines for you to follow.

**TABLE 0.3** Case Analysis Evaluation

| *Suggested Criteria* | *Poor, Weak, Needs Improvement* | *Satisfactory, Acceptable, Good* | *Outstanding, Exemplary, Excellent* |
|---|---|---|---|
| Thoroughness | One or more required section is missing or treated perfunctorily<br>X points | All required sections are addressed to a great extent<br>X points | All required sections are addressed completely<br>X points |
| Theoretical Relevance | The analysis does not incorporate relevant theories<br>X points | Addresses theories and course concepts appropriately<br>X points | Addresses theories and concepts appropriately and insightfully<br>X points |
| Quality of Analysis | Does not suggest careful thought or provide insights<br>X points | Analysis suggests both effort and understanding of the material<br>X points | Detailed analysis that offers careful and logical inferences<br>X points |
| Conclusions or Implementation | Unsupported or missing arguments overlook salient issues<br>X points | Supported arguments capture main issues<br>X points | Supported arguments address both main issues and subtle or secondary problems<br>X points |
| Writing Quality | Careless writing, many grammar and spelling errors, poor organisation<br>X points | Clear writing, few grammar and spelling errors, organised presentation<br>X points | Flawless writing, clear organisation, correct grammar and spelling<br>X points |

## APPENDIX 5 SELF-GRADING RUBRIC

Use this rubric to evaluate the quality of your own work before you hand it in.

**TABLE 0.4** Self-Grading Rubric

| | *Something Is Wrong* | *Everything Is Correct* | *Student Comment Here* |
|---|---|---|---|
| Presence of all required elements (refer to original assignment) | What is missing? Add it. | In the column to the right, list the items that appear in the Table of Contents. | |
| Issues | Some primary or secondary issues are missing. | All the primary and secondary issues have been dealt with and prioritised. | . |
| Adequacy of discussion of consequences, depth of data analysis, application of theory | Weak in one or more of the listed areas. | Issues are fully developed, including alternatives, consequences clearly spelled out, data analysis is comprehensive, and theory is applied correctly. | . |
| Quality of expression | I have not run Spell Check or Grammar Check. I have not had someone else proofread my work. | My work has been proofread by someone else, and all errors have been corrected. | |
| Would I be willing to turn in this report to my employer? | If no – fix it! | If yes, you're done. Hand it in. | |
| What grade would you give this project? | C or less | A or B | |

# PART 1

# Resilience and Recovery

The cases in this part reflect the diversity in the tourism and hospitality industry and the resilience of SMEs. The cases reflect 1) the onset of the pandemic 2) during the pandemic, or, 3) during the recovery phase. The COVID-19 related cases offer a 'window' on what was happening in some SMEs. This was a period of unprecedented uncertainty and disruption that has transformed the sector in all respects.

DOI: 10.4324/9781003280040-3

# CASE 1

## PIVOTING IN THE TOURISM SECTOR

### COVID-19

*Rebecca Wilson-Mah and Katherine MacRae*

**Synopsis**

Maple Leaf Adventures offered small ship cruises and multi-day excursions in Canada's spectacular coastal locations on the west coast of British Columbia. On April 8, Kevin Smith reflected on the seismic change that had occurred over the space of four weeks and the onset of the COVID-19 pandemic. Smith needed a completely new plan for his business. He was also concerned about the other small business partners he worked with on BC's west coast, and what was ahead for these SMEs and their partnerships. This case supports business and tourism students at the undergraduate and graduate level to identify the content and process of possible pivots for a small or medium enterprise and the possibilities that can be developed when SMEs and their representative associations work together.

On April 8, 2020, Kevin Smith, the owner of Maple Leaf Adventures, headquartered in Victoria, BC, thought back to when tourism was flourishing. The Maple Leaf Adventures brand was established and represented an extraordinary ecotourism experience in a marine environment. Smith had spent much of the morning reflecting on March 12, the date that British Columbia, a Canadian province with 22.1 million arrivals, had closed its borders. Smith remembered how he had focused on the news from early March. He had listened to what the Health Minister, Adrian Dix, and the Provincial Health Officer, Dr. Bonnie Henry, along with the Prime Minister of Canada, Justin Trudeau, said about COVID-19. Smith still found it hard to come to terms with the change that had happened since early March. All trips had been booked, with the crew packed and ready to shove off. The small ship marine tour operators had been in for a banner season with sold-out trips, great crew, and a summer of adventures that made sailing the coast of Alaska and British Columbia "Super, Natural"™. Today, less than a month later, he needed a plan. He was stuck and very concerned about his business and his employees. He needed to do something to pivot his business and needed to do it now.

#### The Past Month

Over the past month Smith had spent each waking moment trying to figure out how this new virus would impact his tourism business. Maple Leaf Adventures and other marine tour operations were learning quickly that refunds to guests due to trip cancellations and

DOI: 10.4324/9781003280040-4

closing parts of the tour season were needed. Faced with a new operating issue every day, Smith reflected that he was in the greatest challenge of his career as a small ship tour operator. Parks where he operated his trips had also closed. Today, First Nation communities where his boats operated had closed their communities. People throughout British Columbia were told to hunker down and not go anywhere. And the worst part for Smith was the uncertainty.

An added burden was deciding when to cancel trips that were booked and paid for. Operations for remote small ship trips had begun months in advance and had included: secured park use permits, collaboration with First Nations, the scheduling of trips, aligning crew schedules, and communicating with guests about trip preparedness (Exhibit 1.1). Well before that, key overhead and capital spending had occurred and had included expensive winter maintenance, as well as ongoing marketing, communicating with other stakeholders involved, transportation, arrangements for hotels for pre- and post-trip stays for guests, and orders with food and beverage suppliers. Smith also thought about all the pre-work and investment that had already gone into making the 2020 season a success and associated worries about his insurance policy and if the pandemic would be covered. He, as well as several colleagues, had also recently invested millions of dollars in expansion projects, and these capital costs were meant to be paid down over several years. Significant decisions had to be made on how to support his team, who were now in a precarious position due to the potential of significant trip cancellations. He needed to find a way to keep them working in the industry (and not switch careers) so that these very skilled employees would be available when a restart happened. Smith had trust that their exceptional guest relations focus would help them continue to foster loyalty.

## Maple Leaf Adventures

Maple Leaf Adventures was a small ship tour operator known for taking guests to remote places on the British Columbia and Alaska coast. An old friend of Smith's had owned the SV Maple Leaf and was one of the first people to explore the coast as a tourism company. Seeing the success, Smith purchased Maple Leaf Adventures in 2001 and had worked tirelessly building relationships with competitors and other tourism operators, as well as First Nations communities and conservation organisations along the coast. He had also worked hard to build different industry associations. He believed that there was an advantage to having an industry voice lobby on your businesses behalf. Maple Leaf Adventures had three boats: a 138-foot Catamaran Cascadia; Swell, an 88-foot Tug; and Maple Leaf a 92-foot Schooner. The boats were of heritage design with advanced equipment to make the boats as environmentally friendly as possible. Operations for the marine tourism industry typically ran between March and October, with closure in winter due to the roughness of the seas and the weather on the west coast of British Columbia. Maple Leaf Adventures held a reputation as a leader in ecotourism and was a founding member of the Gwaii Haanas Tour Operators Association, Commercial Bear Viewing Association (CBVA), and Small Ship Tour Operators Association, as well as an executive member of the Wilderness Tourism Association of BC (Exhibit 1.2).

On April 8, 2020, Maple Leaf Adventures employed 12 full time staff and over 60 part time seasonal crew, all experts in their fields as naturalists, chefs, captains, and bear viewing guides. With guests coming from all parts of the world, Maple Leaf Adventures prided itself on being an ambassador to the coast and welcomed people from Canada, the United States of America, United Kingdom, Australia, and many other countries. Trips ranged anywhere from five to ten days and averaged approximately $8,000 per person.

## Smith's Approach to Working in the Coastal Marine and Land Environment

With a history of working on the coast, Smith knew when he bought Maple Leaf Adventures 20 years earlier, he was going to give back to the marine ecosystem. As a backcountry/marine park ranger for a decade, Smith had always given extra effort to protect and educate about the environment, from bears to beach clean-ups. He worked hard over the 20 years to build a successful company, one that was known to be a steward of the land and sea, and that worked ethically for the environment. Another part that Smith was proud of was the relationships he formed with First Nations communities over the years. These relationships were not only important to his operation but important to those in whose traditional territory he was operating.

Years before the British Columbia government legislated the United Nations Declaration of the Rights of Indigenous People (UNDRIP), Smith, along with other small ship tour operators, approached First Nations in the Great Bear Rainforest to establish protocol agreements governing their tourism operations in those territories. These agreements recognised it was the Nations' territory, and they set up economic benefits to the communities' stewardship programs (like taxes the companies pay), as well as agreements on stewardship and employment. Smith had stepped forward and sought permission from the Coastal First Nations and developed what was known as protocol agreements to work in traditional territory. Smith knew that he had to look past his own needs for a successful operation and look to see what would help to make others successful as well.

While sitting on his deck thinking about his company and employees, Smith said, "*There has to be something we can do to make it through this!*"

At that moment, Smith realised that Maple Leaf Adventures was probably going to lose the business season ahead. Smith also recognised that a way ahead was one he would not be able to figure out for his business alone.

## The Eco-Tourism Community in BC's West Coast

The ecotourism entrepreneurs and association members all shared a passion for the marine environment. This passion had been a driving force in the life choices they had made and how they had created their businesses, and was a shared value deeply held by all. As eco-tourism businesses they had expertise that could be used to fund other provincially or federally funded projects for the public good. The eco-tourism businesses provided attractive future growth potential as well as jobs, social and environmental responsibility, and prestige for Canada.

Smith always believed that small businesses needed to work together, and past projects with the Wilderness Tourism Association of British Columbia (WTABC) and the CBVA proved that when multiple businesses work together, things happened (Exhibit 1.2). In 2016 the CBVA, while working collaboratively with other groups, successfully closed the grizzly bear hunt in British Columbia. Smith worked closely with Kathy MacRae,

Executive Director for the CBVA, an accomplished lobbyist who had been integral to the grizzly bear hunt closure (Exhibit 1.3). From this experience, he knew her contacts in the government ran deep and he could gain from her expertise. Smith, as the President of the WTABC, worked with Scott Benton, Executive Director for the WTABC (Exhibit 1.3), also a former senior-level manager for BC Parks. Smith knew that his experience managing government contracts would be invaluable, and his relationships with the different First Nations would be another piece to this puzzle. Smith had advocated for years for working protocol agreements with First Nations and a relationship that would be mutually beneficial; now was no different.

Smith wondered if he could find some way forward, including his contacts and not have to work alone. He needed to find a plan to save his business because there was no hope in sight of COVID-19 going away. Smith wanted to get something started, so on April 8, 2020, he picked up the phone and called his colleague Russell Markel, owner of Outer Shores Expeditions (Exhibit 1.3). As seasonal marine tourism operators, their window of opportunity was small, so any plan was weather-dependent. They talked about their crews, who suddenly did not have jobs, and most likely would not because of the seasonal aspect of their businesses. The hardest part for the coastal marine operators was the uncertainty. No one knew what the future was going to hold.

Smith and Markel decided they needed to bring all stakeholders together and fast so they could build on their strong connections and trust to explore options together. All the stakeholders needed to have a hand in identifying and navigating potential new paths for mutual benefit. How might they pivot?

**Discussion Questions**

1 What are the external, global changes that have made the operating environment for this business unpredictable, and what were the effects of these changes on the business?
2 What are the pros and potential cons that you can associate with owning and operating Maple Leaf Adventures during the COVID-19 pandemic?
3 What are the pivot options for Maple Leaf Adventures?
4 As the owner of an SME, what might prevent or stall Smith from pivoting the business?

**Learning Activity**

Guillén, M. F. (2020). How businesses have successfully pivoted during the pandemic. *Harvard Business Review*. Retrieved November 21, 2020, from: https://hbr.org/2020/07/how-businesses-have-successfully-pivoted-during-the-pandemic

Read the article by Guillén (2020): How businesses have successfully pivoted during the pandemic.

In this article, Guillén (2020) proposed that a pivot should meet the following three conditions:

1 Align the firm with one or more of the long-term trends created or intensified by the pandemic, including remote work, shorter supply chains, social distancing, consumer introspection, and enhanced use of technology.

2 Create a lateral extension of the firm's existing capabilities, cementing, and not undermining its strategic intent.
3 Offer a sustainable path to profitability, one that preserves and enhances brand value in the minds of consumers (Guillén, 2020 para 11–13)

Create a mind map that captures the different ways that Maple Leaf Adventures can create a three-condition pivot. Be sure to come up with as many ways as possible to respond to each of the conditions for a pivot and to capture all these ideas in the mind map.

Questions to consider that align with the three conditions identified by Guillén (2020):

1 Name three societal trends that may inform the options available in this case and explain each one.
2 List the current capabilities that reflect the strategic intent of these coastal businesses and associations. Name three lateral extensions that you consider feasible.
3 Consider your response, name, and then explain your first choice of pivot option.

## Acknowledgement

Kevin Smith and the case authors acknowledge that this case is a shared story about five entrepreneurs – Kevin Smith, Russell Markel, Randy Burke, Ross Campbell, and Eric Boyum – and the First Nation communities of Kitasoo Xai's/xais, Gitga'at, Heiltsuk, Wuikinuxv, and Nuxalk.

## References and Suggested Reading

Guillén, M. F. (2020). How businesses have successfully pivoted during the pandemic. *Harvard Business Review, 7.*

Kamaludin, M. F., Xavier, J. A., & Amin, M. (2022). Social entrepreneurial sustainability during the COVID-19 pandemic. *Social Enterprise Journal, 18*(2), 344–363.

Kirtley, J., & O'Mahony, S. (2023). What is a pivot? Explaining when and how entrepreneurial firms decide to make strategic change and pivot. *Strategic Management Journal, 44*(1), 197–230.

Thukral, E. (2021). COVID-19: Small and medium enterprises challenges and responses with creativity, innovation, and entrepreneurship. *Strategic Change, 30*(2), 153–158.

## Exhibits

**Exhibit 1.1** Operational Characteristics for Maple Leaf Adventures and Outer Shore Expeditions

| Operational Characteristics | Maple Leaf Adventures | Outer Shores Expeditions |
|---|---|---|
| **Number of vessels** | 3 | 1 |
| **Number of full-time employees** | 12 | 2 |
| **Number of part-time employees** | 60+ | 2 |
| **Technical equipment** | Schooner, Tugboat, Catamaran, 4 zodiacs, 2 landing craft, office space, dock space, | Schooner, zodiac, office space (released during COVID-19), dock space |
| **Background** | 20 + years of operation | Since 2011 |
| **Prior to the pandemic, bookings for 2020** | Sold Out | Sold Out |
| **Revenue loss at onset of pandemic on April 8, 2020** | Loss of 100% revenue | Loss of 100% revenue |
| **Clients** | Canada, USA, UK, Australia | Canada, USA, UK, Australia |
| **Trip duration** | Average 5–10 days | Average 5–10 days |
| **Trip cost** | Average $8,000 per person | Average $5,000 per person |

Source: Table developed by authors from primary research with Kevin Smith.

**Exhibit 1.2** Tourism Associations

| |
|---|
| **Small Ship Tour Operators Association** – The Small Ship Tour Operators Association of British Columbia had seven members, all of them 100% Canadian owned and operated, small-ship based travel companies. These operators specialised in providing niche wilderness travel experiences for small groups of 6–24 passengers, along the British Columbia and Alaska coastline. They operated in the Vancouver Island, Haida Gwaii, and Great Bear Rainforest regions. This association formalised the way these colleagues have historically worked together to solve issues greater than themselves. The Association members were Kevin Smith, Maple Leaf Adventures; Randy Burke, Bluewater Adventures; Russell Markel, Outershores Expeditions; Ross Campbell, Mothership Adventures; and Eric Boyum, Ocean Adventures. |

(*Continued*)

**Exhibit 1.2** (Continued)

| |
|---|
| **Wilderness Tourism Association** – The Wilderness Tourism Association of British Columbia (WTABC) supported BC's world-class wilderness-based tourism operators. Working with industry, government, and non-government organisations, the association addressed threats and opportunities for a healthy industry and environment. Specific areas of advocacy and policy development included forestry stewardship, pipelines, land tenures and open-net salmon farms, strategic alliances with government and tourism organisations, and ongoing communication with wilderness tourism operators. The association included wilderness tour companies, destination marketing operators, and wilderness tourism industry experts. The WTABC assisted tour operators to address threats and opportunities. |
| **Commercial Bear Viewing Association** – The Commercial Bear Viewing Association of British Columbia (CBVA) was formed to promote sustainable bear viewing in British Columbia and aid in the protection of wild bears and their ecosystems. The CBVA was committed to continuing to update bear viewing techniques and strategies and develop a guide certification program and professional research on human–bear interactions. |

Source: Author's and primary interview data from Kevin Smith.

**Exhibit 1.3** Small Ship Tour Operators and Association Members for the Wilderness Tourism Association of BC and the Commercial Bear Viewing Association

| |
|---|
| **Maple Leaf Adventures** – Owner and Captain Kevin Smith had over 20 years of experience, including coordinating remote beach clean-ups on north-western Vancouver Island for BC Parks, working as a fisheries patrol officer and backcountry park ranger, and Maple Leaf Adventures celebrated 20 years in operation in 2021. |
| **Outer Shores Expeditions** – Owner and Captain Russell Markel had a PhD in marine ecology and extensive experience leading and coordinating large interdisciplinary projects. Markel was owner and captain of the 70-foot Schooner Passing Cloud. Outer Shores employed two full-time employees and two seasonal employees. It was a small yet significant tourism provider for these small ship tours. |
| **Bluewater Adventures** – Owner and Captain Randy Burke had a degree in education and extensive experience taking guests on adventures along the BC and Alaska coast. He had sailed across the Atlantic and Pacific on tall ships. Burke was an outward-bound instructor with a 500-ton master's license to captain large boats. |
| **Mothership Adventures** – Owner and Captain Ross Campbell was a former tugboat captain with 17 years' experience as a helicopter pilot. Since 2005 he had skippered the Columbia III in summer and upgraded her in the winter. He was familiar with the BC coast, and like the other small ship tour operators, he made safety a priority. |
| **Ocean Adventures** – Owner and Captain Eric Boyum cared deeply about humans, animals, and the flora and fauna. The Great Bear II offered trips to remote and spectacular settings on BC's coast. Qualified and experienced Boyum educated guests on coastal ecosystems. |
| **Scott Benton** – Executive Director of the Wilderness Tourism Association. Since 2016, Benton was actively involved in resource, recreation, and tourism management in British Columbia for over 30 years. He had previously worked for the Province of BC in technical, management, and senior management positions responsible for environmental management, land use planning, |

(*Continued*)

**Exhibit 1.3** (Continued)

| |
|---|
| and parks governance and management. Benton was passionate about working with people to create practical solutions for positive social, environmental, and economic outcomes. |
| **Katherine MacRae** – Executive Director for the Commercial Bear Viewing Association of BC. With over 30 years of experience in the tourism industry and a master of arts in Tourism Management from Royal Roads University, MacRae brought a passion for the industry to everything she did. Through MacRae's work, she was a strong advocate for wildlife in BC and was instrumental in closing the grizzly bear hunt in December 2017. |

Source: Author's summary.

# CASE 2

## A CASE OF RESILIENCE AND AGILITY

### The Craigdarroch Castle

*Rebecca Wilson-Mah and Giovanni Malcolm*

**Synopsis**

The Craigdarroch Castle was a non-profit tourist attraction and a national historic site. The attraction operated solely on memberships, donations, special events, and admission fees. In March 2020, as COVID-19 became a public health emergency, John Hughes, Executive Director, announced that The Craigdarroch Castle was closed until further notice. This decision was made to protect the health and safety of staff, volunteers, and the community. Hughes realised he needed a process and framework that would help him and the team adapt to the operating restrictions and all the operational changes needed to respond to COVID-19.

In the winter of 2020, grave concerns were rapidly intensifying around the globe about a new strain of coronavirus called COVID-19. On March 12, 2020, John Hughes, Executive Director of The Craigdarroch Castle, located in Victoria, BC, Canada, participated in a lengthy board meeting. The meeting had been called to discuss the implications of the new coronavirus, and the outcome was the difficult decision to close The Craigdarroch Castle [henceforth, the Castle]. That same day, and to reflect a little, Hughes walked around the Castle grounds and took in the magnificent view of the ocean and mountains. The normalcy of his routine was a way to stay calm on this atypical day for which, Hughes reflected, the sunshine seemed altogether unsuitable. In his 13 years of working at the Castle, the heritage museum had only closed for three days each year, and from March 16, it would be closed to visitors for an uncertain length of time. COVID-19 was all Hughes could think about. He was deeply concerned about the impending closure of the Castle and the current absence of an operational plan. Hughes determined he needed to bring his management team together and create a nimble and action-oriented way to both plan and make decisions effectively.

DOI: 10.4324/9781003280040-5

Hughes had a lot of questions to ask himself. He was unsure as to what the strategy would be to keep people employed and keep the Castle going. How would he lead a team that had never worked virtually before, how would he keep track of the team, and how could the Castle continue to operate in the virtual space (Exhibits 2.1 and 2.2). He worried about how to continue to earn an income for the Castle and how to track projects. What would be the strategy? To compound matters, the expenses would remain relatively the same, without income from admissions.

### Giovanni Malcolm

Saddened about the loss of guests and all the daily activities and liveliness within the castle, Hughes reached out to Giovanni Malcolm, Operations & Development Manager. Malcolm had joined The Craigdarroch Castle a year earlier and had considerable experience leading in complex situations. He was a change management practitioner with over 10 years in HR and business strategy and held a MA graduate degree in tourism management. His main responsibilities were to lead the Castle team of about 25 full- and part-time employees, plus over 50 volunteers. Later that day Hughes sent Malcolm an email:

> This closure is not going to be easy. I'm going to miss this. I enjoy hearing the numerous radio calls for reinforcement, the laughter, the looks of astonishment and wonder at the woodwork, or the discovery of the 17 fireplaces throughout the castle floors. I enjoy seeing the faces of the children as they listen to stories by our expert storytellers and the look of relief on the parents' faces, content that they have made the right choice on visiting. I will even miss hearing the constant reminders to visitors that they cannot touch the artifacts and having to explain this for the 23rd time on any given day.

Shifting to the major task at hand, Hughes further stated,

> Giovanni, I'm interested in your perspective on how we should proceed and lead through this crisis – we need to work together and lean on each other.

### John Hughes

John Hughes was the kind of leader who led from the front, with a very hands-on approach, and he could be seen preparing for board meetings one minute and, "if needs be," mopping floors the next minute. His office sat at the top of the office stairs, with his door always open ready to meet and greet each employee and volunteer. He had a personal connection with each of the employees and looked forward to chatting with the volunteers when they came in. He frequently stated to staff and volunteers,

> Every day feels like a new way to make magical experiences for our guests, and you all play such a pivotal role in this endeavour; we really appreciate all of you.

Hughes had moved to Vancouver Island over 30 years earlier and was a true Vancouver Island tourism expert. He had joined the Castle 18 years ago as the Operations Manager, before being promoted to his current role as Executive Director in 2010. Prior to joining the Castle as Operations Manager and before becoming the Executive Director, Hughes had owned his own business. He understood the nuts and bolts of the tourism industry very well, and he kept in touch with the tourism and heritage sector through active participation in networking events, memberships, conventions, and other direct connections with industry professionals.

### Victoria's Tourism Industry

Located in Victoria, British Columbia, Canada, the Castle was part of a tourism sector that was a major contributor to the economy in Victoria. Victoria welcomed visitors from Canada and from the United States, Europe, and Asia, with a growing market from the Caribbean and South America. With many natural and built attractions, beaches, trails, and parks, Victoria was a favourite spot for visitors for short stays in all seasons. The cruise ship industry contributed significantly to the tourism economy in Victoria. Many businesses and not-for-profit museums and heritage sites in Victoria depended on passengers from the seasonal cruise ship season and the income that they generated. The closure of the cruise industry was a dramatic reminder of the extensive reach of COVID-19 in the tourism sector and local economy (Exhibit 2.1).

### The Craigdarroch Castle

The Craigdarroch Castle was a national historic site built between 1887 and 1890 by the coal magnate Robert Dunsmuir. The attraction was often described as Canada's Castle and represented a colonial Victorian history. The Castle's website described it as "a shining example of a bonanza castle built by entrepreneurs who became wealthy during the industrial era." The Castle was a non-profit organisation, and operations were financed solely by memberships, donations, special events, and admissions fees. The Castle did not receive funding from the government and operated largely on admissions from Canadian guests and international visitors. The Dunsmuir family sold The Craigdarroch Castle in 1909, and it was privately owned. Between 1919 and 1921 the Castle was owned by the Bank of Montreal and then between 1919 and 1921, right after World War I, it was used as a military hospital. It also served as a college, a music conservatory, and offices for one of Victoria's school boards. In 1969 James Nesbitt, a local newspaper man, took a radical initiative to complete a heritage restoration of the Castle to reflect the days of the Dunsmuir family. Since the 1970s The Craigdarroch Castle Historical Museum Society has owned and operated the Castle. The Castle had a website that explained the history of the site[1].

The Castle employed 16 full- and part-time staff, and up to 15 casual staff, along with over 50 volunteers, who had dedicated shifts every week (Exhibit 2.3). The annual revenue was in the region of \$2.4 million dollars with a combination of admission sales of around 1.6 million, museum store sales of approximately \$400,000, and other revenue that included: memberships, rental income, or cash donations. Expenses were approximately 2.2 million, with the largest chunk going to salaries at around 1.1 million dollars; property operating expense of around \$300,000; office expenses of around \$100,000; and other expenses that included: curatorial expense, insurance, professional fees, and cost of goods sold.

## The Visitor Experience

Advertised as a tourist attraction, the museum received visitors from all over the world, however, predominantly from Europe, China, the United States, and Mexico. There were the locals, too, who would come by, either from word of mouth, through their interest in the "castle on the hill," as museum members, or on school trips. Visitors came either on their own accord, through a local tour agency, or from the cruise ships that docked in Victoria over the spring, summer, and early autumn months.

On the nights that cruise ships were in the Victoria Inner Harbour, the Castle remained open until 11 pm. Visitors entered the Visitor Centre, where they either purchased a ticket or validated their tickets with a staff member and were given a map of the museum, a brochure, an "I-Spy" scavenger hunt for children, and the option of renting an audio tour. The visitors then wandered the Visitor Centre, read some background historical information posted throughout, and visited the gift shop, before heading to the front door of the castle.

At the Castle front door, a staff member greeted them and instructed them on how to use the shoe cleaner to protect the historic carpets and floors. They also instructed the visitor on the rules to follow while inside, which were:

> Respect the barriers. Refrain from touching the artifacts. Take as many photos as you please; yes, flash photography is allowed. All children must remain supervised. No running. We love questions, so if you have one, please ask any of our staff or volunteers.

The visitors, with or without an audio tour, made their way through the castle, floor by floor, using the main staircase. Once on the fourth floor, after visiting the tower, they then proceeded down another staircase to see the second side of the home before exiting through the back door located in the original kitchen. The Castle library was one of the first where visitors interacted with staff.

The organisation of the visitor experience relied on physical interaction, and every point of the visitor experience was face to face. Throughout the castle, visitors interacted with text plaques in each room, and volunteers and docents were eager to answer any questions the visitors might happen upon. After exiting the museum, many would wander back around the building towards the Visitor's Centre again, use the washrooms, and browse the gift shop.

The entire visit lasted about an hour and a half. If they were really interested, then there were times when they would have visitors staying in the museum for up to three hours. If the visitors came during a special event or time of the year, they might happen upon musical or theatrical performances, festive decorations, special events, and/or family programming. Christmas was a magical time of year for the Castle, and it came alive with decorations, volunteers and visitors carolling in the drawing room, and different musicians playing throughout the season. If the day was nice, they might take time to walk around or relax on the South Lawn. In summer months they could purchase food from the museum's seasonal concession, before heading back down the hill towards their next activity, accommodation, or home.

### Building Visitation and Current Marketing

As the Castle was largely dependent on foot traffic, the website was not fully equipped to present virtual tours or other offerings in the digital space. The Castle had started to generate a presence on Facebook and Instagram and had a substantial database accessible to the public where subscribers could read about the artifacts and take a mini tour. For years, the Castle had planned on increasing its digital footprint, and had even hired outside consultants to create a digital strategy for the Castle. The recommendations had not been implemented, and the report findings were available for reference. There were marketing plans for blog posts, podcasts, mini tours, and a Curator's Corner, where the public could pose questions, generate content, and build a community of passionate advocates. The Castle had an advertising firm, and did most of its marketing in visitor centres, BC Ferries, hotels, and local tourism outlets.

### Gift Shop Operations

The Craigdarroch Castle Gift Shop, located in the museum's Visitor Centre, was run by the Gift Shop Manager with the help of one or two part-time staff or volunteers. Visited by guests often before and after their time in the museum, the shop offered items such as souvenirs, Canada- and Victoria-themed souvenirs, as well as a selection of locally made collectables and consumables (artwork, accessories, teas, chocolates, etc.). The Gift Shop Manager, who purchased products and managed inventory, was credited for transforming the gift shop into a place that appealed to both tourists and locals for its variety in product. Over 85% of the gift shop sales were from visitors who came on tours at the Castle. The Gift Shop conducted online sales through Shopify, but pushing online sales was never a strategic imperative for the store. Therefore, there was no big push to acquire sales through this method.

### Finding a Way Forward

Hughes realised quickly that he needed to keep The Craigdarroch Castle alive – and he needed a process and framework that would help him and the team identify what to do. Within seven days, Hughes had to come up with a plan to present to the board to 1) keep people employed; 2) keep employees occupied; 3) design a tracking tool to gauge progress; 4) decide who could come into the office and who should work remotely; and 5) decide how long the company could afford to keep staff employed if the situation did not change. His end goal was to have an operating attraction by November 2020.

Hughes was uncertain about the approaches that were needed for him to guide the operation in these extraordinary circumstances. This was all new territory, and he knew analysis and decisions needed to happen fast – he did not have much time to dwell or ponder. He needed to bring the team together and re-imagine the very core of the visitor experience. He reflected on the relatively "old fashioned" operating model that the Castle relied on. What could it become, and how to get it there? There was a lot to get done, and most staff would need to work remotely (Exhibit 2.4).

**Discussion Questions**

1. What are the projects that Hughes should focus on first for The Craigdarroch Castle –can you explain your choices?
2. What possibilities should Hughes consider that keep employees employed and occupied and are also aligned with the museum's purpose and functions?
3. In this situation that Hughes was in, what kinds of tools and approaches would you consider helpful for virtual planning?
4. What tracking tools could Hughes use to create a plan for the Castle in this crisis, and what is the one you would recommend?

**Learning Activity**

Bolman, L., & Deal, T. (2017). *Reframing organizations: Artistry, choice and leadership* (6th ed.). Hughes Wiley & Sons.

Bolman and Deal (2017) discuss the importance of reframing, which is the ability to look at situations from more than one angle, with the purpose of developing alternative diagnoses and strategies to move forward. The authors provide four frames to explore organisational situations, to identify corresponding leadership challenges within each of those frames, and to deepen the understanding of the issues, particularly during times of change.

Working with a partner, or in a small team, read Bolman and Deal (2017) and apply each of the frames (HR Focus, Structural Focus, Political Focus, and Symbolic/Systemic Focus) to analyse and recommend strategies for the issues presented as questions below.

**HR Focus**

Question to explore: What would you do to keep people employed and motivated?

**Structural Focus**

Question to explore: What innovative processes/procedures can be used?

**Political Focus**

Question to explore: What is needed to lead in a virtual environment?

**Symbolic/ Systemic Focus**

Question to explore: What would you do to continue to support the tourism industry?

To deepen your learning, share your summaries and seek feedback on them.

## Note

1 Craigdarroch Castle (n.d.). https://thecastle.ca/

## References and Suggested Reading

Bolman, L., & Deal, T. (2017). *Reframing organizations: Artistry, choice and leadership* (6th ed.). Hughes Wiley & Sons.

Booth Sweeney, L., & Sterman, J. D. (2007). Thinking about systems: Student and teacher conceptions of natural and social systems. *The System Dynamics Review*, *23*, 285–312.

Grotzer, T., & Bell Basca, B. (2003). How does grasping the underlying causal structures of ecosystems impact students' understanding? *Journal of Biological Education*, *38*, 16–29.

Oshry, B. (2007). *Seeing systems. Unlocking the mysteries of organizational life.* Berret-Koehler San Francisco.

## Exhibits

**Exhibit 2.1** Communication from Greater Victoria Harbour Authority

From: Greater Victoria Harbour Authority <newsletter@gvha.ca>

Reply-To: Greater Victoria Harbour Authority <newsletter@gvha.ca>
Date: Friday, March 13, 2020 at 9:46 AM
Subject: COVID-19 Cruise Update

Good Morning,
Effective today, Transport Canada has suspended the cruise season across Canada until July 1, 2020.

We respect the decision by the Government of Canada in putting the health and safety of Canadians first. We will work to engage with our cruise partners and terminal operators to comply with the decision.

In dealing with the impact of COVID-19, the health and safety of everyone is always our top concern. While this will have a negative economic impact on our organisation and numerous small businesses and operators in Greater Victoria, we ask that Victorians continue to support dialogue, collaboration, and community through these unprecedented times.

We will remain engaged with Transport Canada, agencies, and other ports across Canada as these regulations are implemented.

Further information regarding COVID-19 and its impacts on port operations in Victoria will continue to be shared here.

The 2020 cruise schedule will continue to be updated as changes occur and is available here.

Thank you,
GVHA

Source: Greater Victoria Harbour Authority with permission.

**Exhibit 2.2** Worksafe BC Announcement

On March 12, 2020, Worksafe BC published their advisory notice for employers and workers to follow that recommended personal hygiene practises and to avoid direct contact with others. All workers who were ill had to stay at home and were advised to contact a healthcare professional. Any worker with the COVID-19 virus was to stay home. If the worker had been outside of Canada within the past 14 days or was in contact with anyone with COVID-19 symptoms or had the virus, they had to remain home and self-isolate until that 14-day period was complete. Worksafe BC advised that an appropriate mask be worn while at work. Additionally, they asked that businesses prepare a continuity and contingency plan, limit worker participation in large social gatherings, consider that workers work remotely, increase workplace cleaning, and take on a new sick leave and compensation policy.

Source: Summarised by the authors from Worksafe BC (n.d.) public announcement on March 12, 2020. https://www.worksafebc.com.

**Exhibit 2.3** Craigdarroch Castle Closure

> Castle Closure due to COVID-19 Precautions
>
> From: Connor Thomas, Receptionist
> Tue 3/17/2020 5:00 PM
>
> Hello,
> Due to the COVID-19 pandemic, The Craigdarroch Castle is closing to protect the health and safety of staff, volunteers, and the community. The Castle will be closed until further notice as of 4:30 p.m., March 16, 2020. As a result, all booked tours have subsequently been cancelled. We're sorry for any disappointment or inconvenience this may have caused. Please respond to this email or phone 250-592-5323 if you have any questions, and we would be happy to reschedule a tour once the situation is ironed out.
>
> Regards,
> Connor

Source: Internal email with permission from The Craigdarroch Castle.

**Exhibit 2.4** Craigdarroch Castle Organisational Chart - March 1, 2020

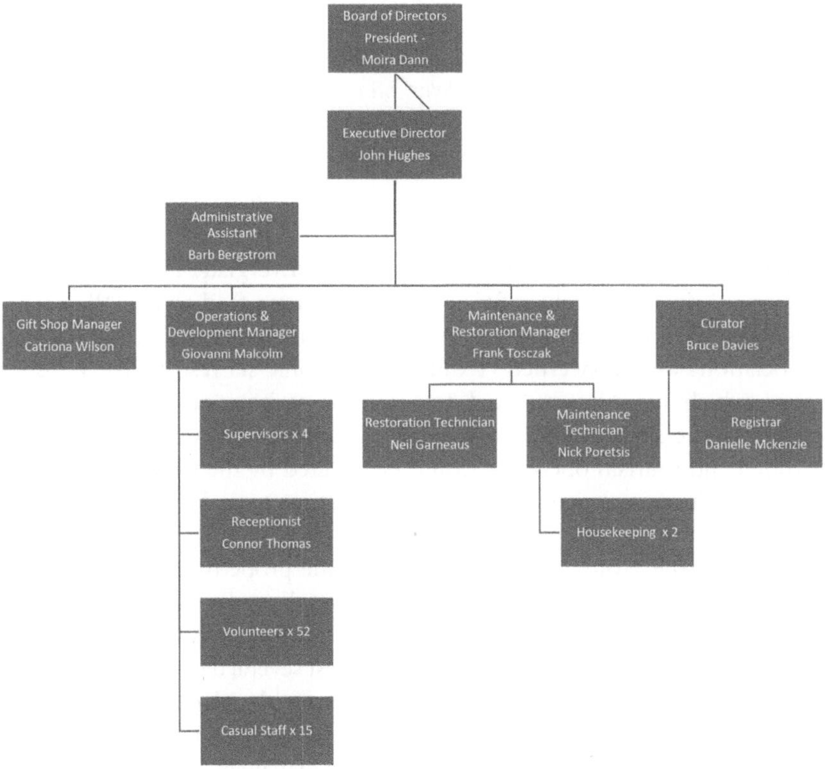


Source: Created by the author with permission from The Craigdarroch Castle.

# CASE 3

## A SUDDEN INHOSPITABLE SITUATION

### The Everglade Hotel

*Rebecca Wilson-Mah and Daniel Bernardes*

**Synopsis**

The Everglade Hotel had just completed a lengthy period of renovations to the public areas, including the lobby and the restaurant. Anticipation was high for a busy summer season, and occupancy rate was forecast to be around 77%. When COVID-19 became a public health issue, the Hotel had to shift gears quickly. With prior experience responding to SARS in a hotel in China, the General Manager looked to Kim Douglas, Director of Rooms, to be a key lead in the response, and Douglas needed to act swiftly.

On March 20, 2020, Kim Douglas, Director of Rooms at the Everglade Hotel (hereafter, the Hotel) in Victoria, British Columbia (BC), checked his news feed again. All accommodations throughout BC faced pandemic-related cancellations and closures, and tourism operators and associations were concerned (Exhibit 3.1). Iconic ski resorts like Whistler Blackcomb Resort, which typically attracted two million visitors per year, had also announced a closure of the ski area and lodging facilities. It was becoming increasingly clear that all BC hotel and tourism operators would be affected by the pandemic. Layoffs and further department closures were imminent, and it was time to make further plans for a closure for the Hotel.

Douglas had worked at the Hotel, a beautiful harbour-side property in tourist-friendly Victoria – for nearly six years. Today, on March 20 the steady stream of bad news had everyone on edge. Most guests had checked out early the previous week, and individual guests and groups had cancelled their reservations over the past several days. With the steady stream of news about the pandemic, the Hotel had quickly created a plan to accommodate guests who could be infected by COVID-19, and on March 13 had developed safety operating procedures. The general manager and the Hotel's management and staff looked

DOI: 10.4324/9781003280040-6

to Douglas to be a key partner to get the next steps right. Douglas considered the support provided by PreparedBC, British Columbia's emergency preparedness education program. Douglas realized that although PreparedBC had encouraged the development of emergency plans for fires, earthquakes, a tsunami, and other scenarios, neither the province nor the Hotel had an emergency plan to guide the Hotel's response to a pandemic (Exhibit 3.2).

### A New Virus

COVID-19 had first caught Douglas' attention in early February 2020 with the alarming news of the spread of the new Coronavirus in Wuhan, China. This new virus had been in the headlines of every news outlet as it spread from China to other countries. In the previous weeks and days, the news had developed at a rapid pace. On March 14, the Federal Government had directed Canadians to avoid travel outside the country and directed Canadians abroad to return immediately. The Federal Government had taken these actions because of an alarming rise of COVID-19 cases in Canada and elsewhere. Douglas thought about the chronology and marveled at the speed of this global crisis. Canada's first COVID-19 case had been reported in late January, and the first case in BC on January 28. The first reported COVID-related death in BC was on March 9, and by March 11 the World Health Organization (WHO) had declared COVID-19 a pandemic (Exhibit 3.3). The news was changing rapidly, and internally at the Hotel, there was a shift in atmosphere that was unmistakable. With cancellations and the pandemic news everywhere, the team was uneasy with the gloomy scenario that was rapidly unfolding.

### From Shanghai to the Everglade Hotel

Growing up in BC, Douglas had always known he wanted a career in hotels. To achieve his goal, he had studied hotel administration at Cornell University, an internationally recognised premier hotel school, graduating with a bachelor of applied science in 2005. Shortly after graduation he began his hotel management career in Shenzhen China, at the Futian Shangri-La Hotel as Executive Assistant Manager for Rooms. At the Futian Shangri-La Hotel he was promoted six times over six years. In 2012 he transferred to Shanghai, to work as Executive Assistant Manager for Rooms at the Pudong Shangri-La. During his tenure in China at the Pudong Shangri-La Douglas had faced a similar epidemic situation with SARS in 2003. In 2014, ready for a change he returned to Canada to take the Director of Rooms position at the hotel.

### Role of Director of Rooms

In his capacity as Director of Rooms, Douglas was responsible for all the departments in the rooms division, which included front office, housekeeping, and maintenance (Exhibit 3.4). Some of his key responsibilities were budgeting, forecasting, developing managers and employees and guest service, while maximizing room revenue and productivity. Douglas was also a key member of the strategic leadership team in the hotel. The Director of Rooms position reflected a second in command position at the hotel. This was not reflected in the organisational chart (Exhibit 3.4); however, it was understood. The General Manager at the Hotel also had the responsibility as Managing Director for a second business owned by the Trust. Given the pandemic emergency and Douglas' expertise, the General Manager had asked Douglas to be very involved in the pandemic response for the Hotel, and to report to him regularly.

## The Everglade Hotel

The Hotel was founded by John and Jennie Anderson in the 1970s. Located by the ocean in Victoria's Inner Harbor, the Hotel had 74 luxury suites and 142 rooms. Until their deaths (John in 2001, and Jennie in 2006), the Andersons had lived on the property and had remained very involved with day-to-day management. Before her death in 2006, Jennie Anderson established a trust to ensure that the hotel would remain intact under independent ownership as a social enterprise. A Trust specified that all hotel profits were to be reinvested in the property.

The Hotel was governed by a Board of Directors. In 2020, the Board consisted of two Internal Directors, the General Manager and Director of Finance, and three external directors. The Hotel employed 112 full-time employees and 45 part-time or seasonal employees. As an independent property all the departments required for the Hotel's operations were on site. The departments were divided into six main areas: accounting, food & beverage, human resources, reservations, rooms division, and sales (Exhibit 3.4). The Hotel had four core hotel values: *excellence, curiosity, respect, and stewardship*. The four values were discussed frequently in all areas of the business, and these values supported decision making and interpersonal communication. These values also represented an appreciation of the significance of a team approach. Douglas believed that the hotel values and team approach were a key part of their success. This success had also been recognised externally through several accomplishments and awards. The Hotel was one of the first carbon neutral hotels in British Columbia (2008) and was recognized as a leader in sustainable business practices. The Hotel also had a Five Green Keys certification[1] awarded in 2015, Ecostar Awards (2015 & 2016), and an Employer of the Year Award (2017).

## Renovations in 2018 and 2019

In 2017 the Board approved an ambitious renovation plan to refurbish the Hotel's public areas and grounds. The years 2018 and 2019 brought some challenges as the renovations took place. The year 2019 had been a year of continuous renovations and several delays. From experience, Douglas knew that renovations in hotels were never easy, and often led to guest complaints about noise, cleanliness issues, and service impairment. To accommodate the renovations the front desk had moved to a temporary location in a corridor, and the meeting spaces had been reduced to make space for the construction. In early February 2020, after working in temporary spaces for a year longer than expected, the Hotel team had been finally able to see the end of the renovations of the public areas, and they had eagerly prepared for a grand reopening. At the beginning of March 2020, 50 events were scheduled for the Hotel, and the summer season was set up to have high occupancy with multiple events and weddings. With the construction completed, 2020 had been set to be best year so far for the hotel. The pandemic uncertainty had changed these expectations, and Douglas was anxious to start planning for possible cancelations or postponements of events and room blocks. This and other pressing decisions were developing at a rapid pace.

## The Tourism Industry

Victoria was a city where tourism had thrived before the pandemic. At Victoria International Airport arrivals had reached 2 million per year. Located in a beautiful, protected harbour, in the heart of Victoria the Hotel was a landmark site. Between 2015 and 2019 (Destination Greater Victoria, 2020) the average accommodation occupancy rate in Victoria was 73.54%.

## Emergency Planning Preparation

According to the BC provincial government's hazard map, the region had possibilities of earthquakes, tsunamis, severe weather, and wildfires. The emergency plan from PreparedBC, had not required tourism operators to account for pandemics in their preparations (Exhibit 3.2). The Hotel had utilised this resource before to develop the emergency plans for earthquake and tsunami. Douglas was acutely aware that the hotel had not developed any emergency plan for a pandemic as a possible threat. Douglas knew that he would have to use all his previous knowledge, leadership skills, and planning expertise to help prepare a response to this imminent threat.

## Time to Close the Hotel

Douglas was very concerned that his division and the Hotel at large was not prepared for this pandemic emergency. He did not have a playbook for this local and global disaster event. There were so many unknowns and no end in sight. Douglas had handled other emergencies before during his career such as SARS in China, but nothing like this. On March 20 it was clear to Douglas that he had to formulate and then swiftly implement an emergency plan to ready the rooms division and other areas of the operation for the closure of the Hotel (Exhibit 3.3). He also wanted to build a contingency plan. The Hotel faced exceptional pandemic-related risk. He knew that his General Manager, and his own direct reports, would soon be looking to him for his operational leadership and agile response, and he wanted to get the next steps right.

### Discussion Questions

1. If Douglas was to recommend a hotel closure, how should he prioritize recommended actions for the Hotel divisions and why? Who should he involve?
2. Name the departments that should remain operational during closure, and explain your reasoning.
3. What actions would be essential during the closure, and how might the response reflect the Hotel's values?
4. What priorities do you recommend that support the Hotel guests and why?
5. What priorities do you recommend that support the Hotel employees and why?
6. Develop a Gantt chart to guide actions and timelines for closure of the Rooms Division.

**Learning Activity: Workplace Health and Safety Agency Regulations and Associated Protocols**

Explore the pandemic-related public health orders and regulations for a healthy and safe workplace. Locate and review some of the workplace health and safety protocols and regulations in your jurisdiction. For example, in BC, Canada, the oversight for workplace health and safety regulations are with an agency called Worksafe BC. The link for this agency is here: https://www.worksafebc.com/en

At the hotel there was a skeleton crew of people who continued to come to work at the hotel. Therefore, those employees had to adapt to the regulations that related to the operation of a hotel.

Answer the following questions:

1 What COVID-19 health and safety protocols did you find?
2 Are there specific protocols for hotels? What are they?
3 If protocols change, what are the implications for the hotel's contingency plan?

Some additional questions:

- What pros and cons do you associate with the General Manager placing significant responsibility to Douglas for the emergency response plan?
- What are the main differences between an emergency response and a contingency plan? Where do you see the opportunities for each to inform the other?
- Reflect on how COVID-19 affected you in your professional life or school life. What are one or two key learnings that you consider to be closely associated with your experience. How might you apply these learnings productively/usefully in the future?

## Note

1 Green Key Global (n.d.) http://www.greenkeyglobal.com/

## References and Suggested Reading


British Columbia. (n.d.). British Columbia hazard map. Retrieved from https://www2.gov.bc.ca/gov/content/safety/emergency-preparedness-response-recovery/preparedbc/know-your-hazards/hazard-map

British Columbia. (2017). PreparedBC: Emergency plan for tourism operators. Retrieved from https://www.go2hr.ca/wp-content/uploads/2017/07/2017-EMBC-Tourism-Plan.pdf

Destination Greater Victoria. (2020). 2019 annual report. Retrieved from https://www.tourismvictoria.com/sites/default/files/dgv_2019_annual_report_web.pdf

Le, D., & Phi, G. (2021). Strategic responses of the hotel sector to Covid-19: Toward a refined pandemic crisis management framework. *International Journal of Hospitality Management*, *94*, 102808–102808. Available at: https://doi.org/10.1016/j.ijhm.2020.102808

McCool, B. N. (2012). The need to be prepared: Disaster management in the hospitality industry. *Journal of Business Hotel Management 1*, *2*(2). Available at: https:/doi:10.4172/2324-9129.1000101

Pforr, C., & Hosie, P. J. (2008). *Crisis management in tourism: Preparing for recovery. Journal of Travel & Tourism Marketing*, *23*(2–4), 249–264.

## Exhibits

### **Exhibit 3.1** Tourism Industry Association of BC: Letter to the Premier of BC

Honourable John Horgan, Premier of BC
PO Box 9041 Stn Prov Govt
Victoria, BC V8W 9E1 March 16, 2020

Re: Tourism Emergency Contingency Fund

Dear Premier Horgan,

As you are aware, the COVID-19 crisis has affected the tourism industry more than any other sector aside from health. Domestic and international travel to British Columbia has virtually been halted. Combined with government's recommendation that residents do not undertake non-essential travel to points outside of Canada, and the corresponding implications on international visitors to BC, the ramifications on our visitor economy are immense.

Given further travel advisories at both the federal and provincial levels, including limiting public gatherings to 250 people and forbidding cruise ships with more than 500 passengers to dock at ports in BC, most travelers have either cancelled visits or are leaving British Columbia for home at a time when the industry is normally building toward its peak season.

To date, several events and conferences of all sizes have either been cancelled or postponed around the province. The domino effect on venues, hotels, restaurants, attractions, suppliers, transportation, and service providers, along with other stakeholders is creating hardships for businesses, employees, and communities throughout British Columbia. In fact, layoffs have already begun or are imminent with many individual tourism sectors.

While the Tourism Industry Association of British Columbia recognizes the need for preventative measures undertaken by provincial and federal health authorities, the uncertainty on present and future edicts, particularly the length and extent of the directives, is causing further difficulties for tourism operators to project, plan and put processes into place to mitigate damage to their businesses, as well as the industry as a whole.

As you know, Tourism is one of BC's top three business sectors, contributing upwards of $19 billion annually in revenues and employing hundreds of thousands of people. In recent years, the industry has set numerous records and up until the COVID-19 crisis, was projected to further grow in 2020. Although tourism is resilient and poised to rebuild after this crisis ends, the length of time the visitor economy recovers to a so-called 'normal' state could take several years. Unfortunately, as an industry largely comprised of small businesses, many operators cannot absorb mounting losses, and aside from laying-off staff, will close their businesses (some permanently) unless government provides stimulus funding, direct financial assistance, or other measures including tax relief.

With new travel restrictions in place, as well as the confirmed and anticipated list of trip and event cancellations, it is estimated that BC's visitor economy will lose in excess of $3 billion in revenue during the March to June period alone. Outside of the healthcare sector, there is no other industry in Canada that is impacted as severely by this mounting crisis than tourism.

Page 2
Premier Horgan

From our scan of destinations around the world, we know that many countries including Australia, New Zealand, Germany, and the United States have already announced stimulus and relief programs ranging from hundreds of millions to several billion dollars to help their respective tourism sectors respond and recover from the impact of COVID-19.

On behalf of British Columbia's 19,000 tourism operators, 330,000 employees, hundreds of industry sectors, communities, and destination marketing organizations, TIABC respectfully requests that the Province of British Columbia take bold, decisive, and meaningful action to support BC's visitor economy.

Premier, thank you for your assistance and for all the steps your government has taken to tackle this extremely serious crisis. TIABC is keen to work with you to develop actions that address the aforementioned issues and opportunities related to BC's visitor economy. I look forward to hearing from you at your earliest convenience.

Best regards,

Walt Judas
CEO, TIABC

Source: Public letter distributed by the Tourism Industry Association of BC (TIABC).

**Exhibit 3.2** PreparedBC Emergency Plan Template for Tourism Operators

PreparedBC

EMERGENCY PLAN FOR TOURISM OPERATORS

This resource is designed to help B.C. tourism businesses and organizations start planning and preparing for emergencies that may impact their staff and guests.

Choose the templates, tools and suggestions that make the most sense for your operation and add to them as needed. One simple step today can make a difference in how effectively you respond to and recover from an emergency. For additional information, review the *PreparedBC: Guide for Tourism Operators* at **www.gov.bc.ca/PreparedBC**.

## RISK AND IMPACT ASSESSMENT

List all the hazards your tourism business might face, including their likelihood and estimated impact.

***Sample:***

| Hazard | Probability | Level of Impact | Potential Impacts |
|---|---|---|---|
| Wildfire | Likely | Severe | ▪ Injury<br>▪ Damage to business infrastructure<br>▪ Disruption to transportation network |

**Probability** = How likely a hazard is to occur (very unlikely, unlikely, possible, likely, very likely)

**Impact** = How big an impact a hazard might have (negligible, low, moderate, significant, severe)

| Hazard | Probability | Level of Impact | Potential Impacts |
|---|---|---|---|
| | | | |
| | | | |
| | | | |
| | | | |
| | | | |

2

Source: British Columbia. (2017). PreparedBC: Emergency plan for tourism operators. Retrieved from https://www.go2hr.ca/wp-content/uploads/2017/07/2017-EMBC-Tourism-Plan.pdf. Public source from The Government of British Columbia.

**Exhibit 3.3** Three-Month Timeline

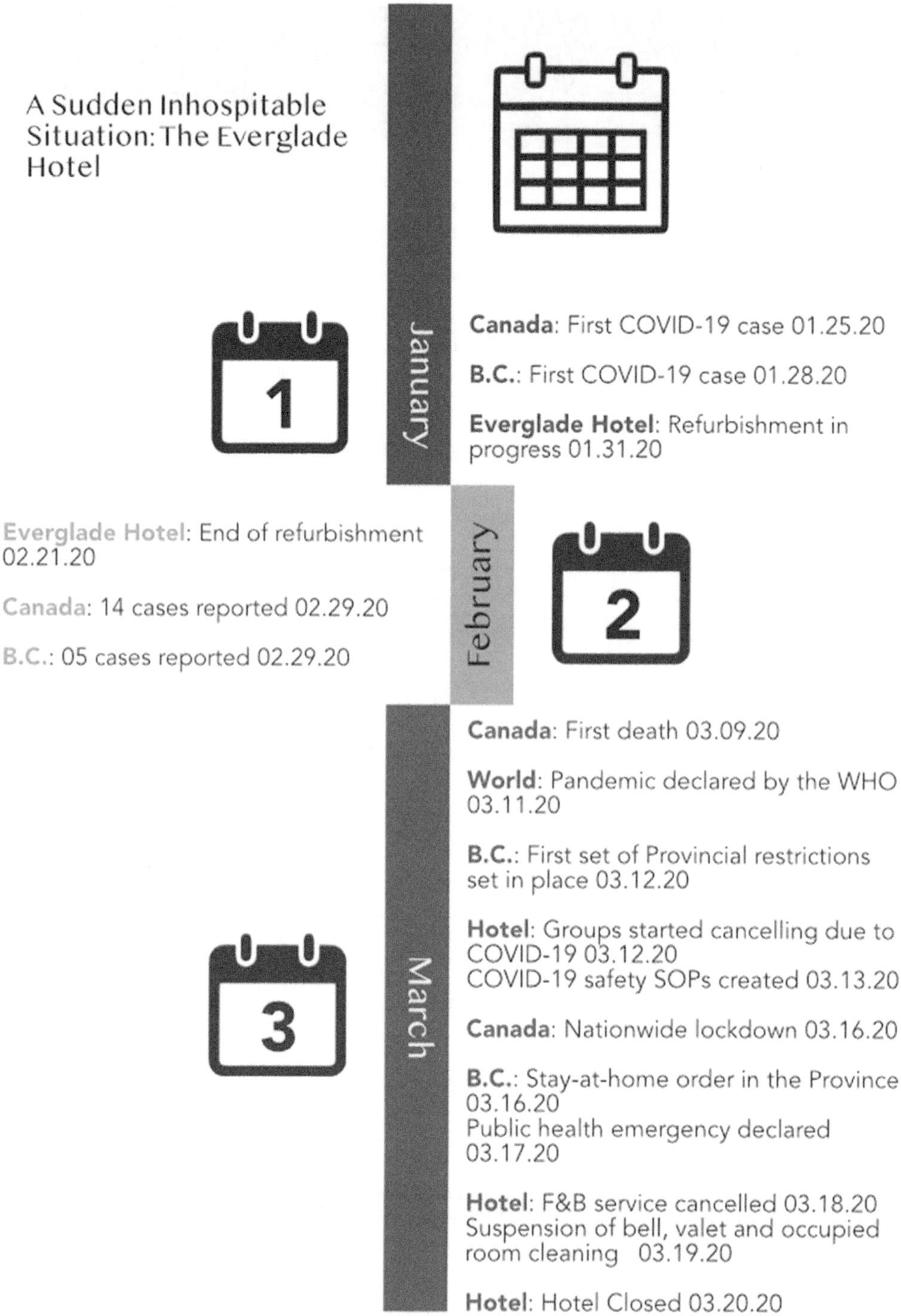


Source: Author's timeline summary.

**Exhibit 3.4** Hotel Organizational Structure

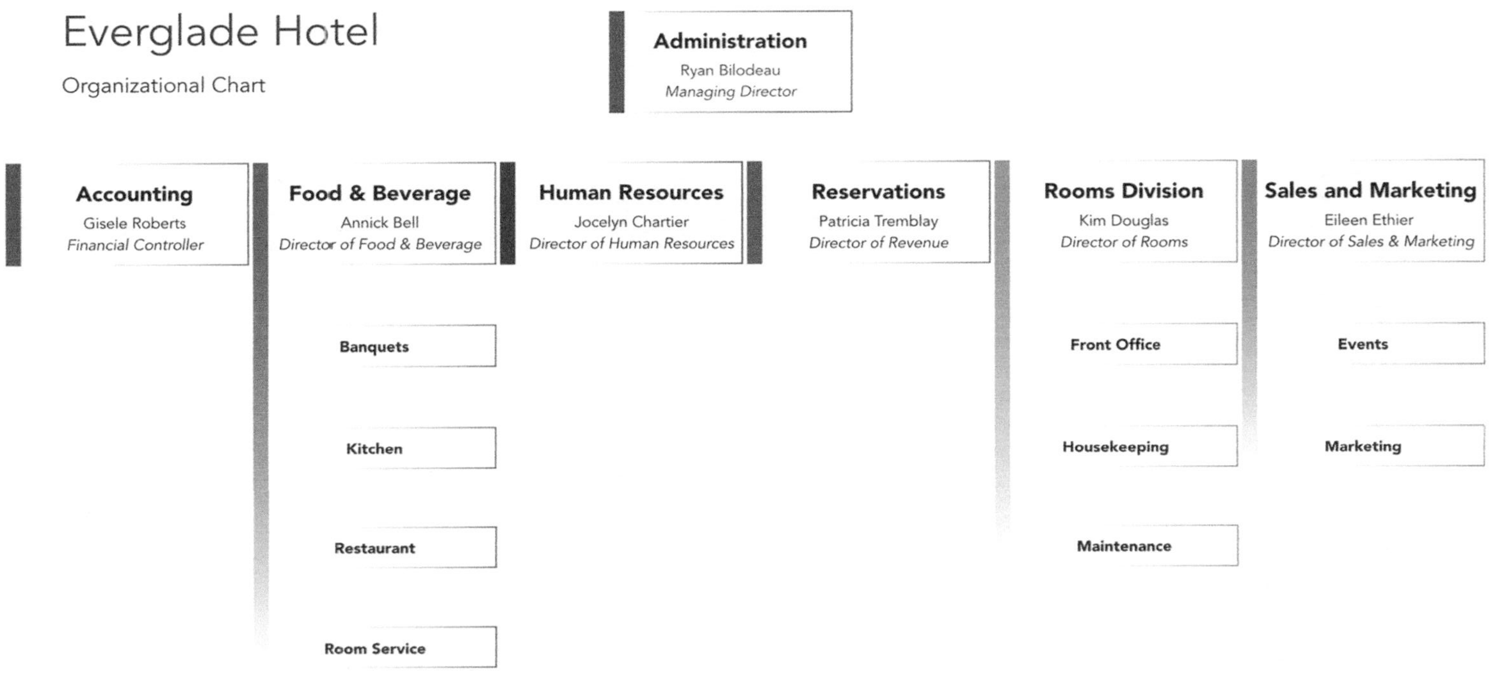


Source: Organizational chart created by authors.

# CASE 4

## TOURISM RESORT EMPLOYERS AND EMPLOYEES ADAPT TO PANDEMIC UNCERTAINTY

*Rebecca Wilson-Mah and Jo Axe*

**Synopsis**

On November 30, 2020, two professors, Sam Brown and Rachel Lee (the researchers), sat down with a virtual coffee over Zoom to review their research data, analysis, and findings. With the onset of the pandemic in March 2020, the tourism industry had been dramatically impacted by COVID-19. In April, the researchers had decided they would help to support tourism employees and employers by studying how employers and employees were experiencing their work environments. They had recently completed the study, based in the tourism town of Whistler, British Columbia (BC, Canada). Lee commented to her colleague, "*Our study has provided evidence of ways that the pandemic has affected how tourism employees work, where they work, and what they expect and need from their employers.*"

With the study close to completion, Brown remarked to Lee that they should now *"focus their work on disseminating their findings and recommendations."* The researchers agreed that there were several recommendations that could be suggested to Whistler's small- and medium-sized employers (SMEs). The data analysis had provided some clear indications related to employee needs and preferences in their workplaces during the pandemic. The challenge ahead was to ensure that these recommendations were presented as actionable steps that employers could consider and use.

### The Research Team

The researchers had collaborated previously on several other projects, and both worked at Royal Roads University in Victoria, British Columbia, Canada. The university had an applied research focus and three research pillars: 1) sustainable communities, livelihoods, and the environment; 2) innovative learning; and 3) thriving organisations. Brown held a PhD

DOI: 10.4324/9781003280040-7

in education, was a Chartered Professional Accountant, and worked in the College of Interdisciplinary Studies. She had recently conducted research with an organisation in Whistler, that used supportive employment techniques to respond to challenges faced by youth who were homeless, or at risk of homelessness. Lee worked in the School of Tourism and Hospitality Management. She held a doctorate in education and an MSc in human resource management, and was a Chartered Professional in Human Resource Management (CPHR). Lee had previous experience in the hotel sector, where she had held different positions in HR with Fairmont Hotels and Resorts, and she continued to hold a deep commitment to research that supported employee engagement and talent development.

## Impact of COVID on Employees in Tourism and Hospitality

Brown and Lee had several connections with employers and employees in Whistler, BC, through their networks and their teaching and research work. The impacts of the pandemic identified in the media and substantiated by their networks included an unstable working environment and related financial stress, job insecurity, and depleted sense of wellbeing. As healthcare professionals had worked to understand the virus and how it was transmitted, workplace occupational health and safety and hygiene protocols had changed frequently in response as more was understood. Health information related to the virus was constantly evolving as employees adjusted to working from home or to working with multiple restrictions in their workplaces. This absence of a deeper understanding of how employees were experiencing uncertainty was the impetus for the data collection the researchers had completed between June 22 and November 24, 2020.

## Employers and Employees in Whistler, BC

In April 2020, close to half the employers in British Columbia lacked confidence[1] that they would be able to re-open post-pandemic, and a similar percentage of small businesses with fewer than five employees had not found federal relief programs helpful. In this pandemic climate, Brown and Lee had approached the Whistler Chamber of Commerce to offer their research services to help support and inform the Chamber members about business adaptation and recovery in the pandemic. Many of the Whistler Chamber members were employers in food and beverage, retail, accommodation, and not-for-profit sectors. The researchers aimed to provide context and data that could support a more optimistic employment climate, with a focus on recovery. Prior to the pandemic, Whistler had had close to 2.5 million annual visitors[2] and fewer than 12,000 permanent residents. If a similar number of visitors resumed after the pandemic restrictions were phased out, and the number of international workers did not return to pre-pandemic levels, tourism SMEs would be in a vulnerable position. Keeping Whistler's current employees engaged and feeling supported was critical to the continued operation of small to midsize tourism organisations in Whistler.

To inform their research, Brown and Lee consulted a Pulse Check Survey conducted by the Whistler Chamber of Commerce with their members and published in July 2020 (Exhibit 4.1). The survey indicated that 27% of employer respondents had seen a 75–100% drop in sales over the preceding two weeks, while 25% of respondents had seen between a 50% and 74% drop in sales. When asked about revenue, 43% of respondents had retained up to 20% of their normal revenue in the preceding 30 days, while only 18% of respondents had retained between 20% and 39% of their normal revenue. Health and safety requirements were significant, and 38% of respondents believed the cost of implementing measures to adhere to health and safety requirements was expensive or very expensive. Staffing was an issue; 43% of businesses had one to five positions unfilled.

## The Research Design – Two Phases

At the beginning of their research, Brown and Lee designed their study in two phases. The researchers believed that it was important to explore both employer and employee perspectives on the COVID-19 work environment in Whistler and the uncertainty created by the pandemic. The first phase of the study, completed in June 2020, focused on how employers were responding to COVID-19 in their businesses in Whistler. The second phase that wrapped up in early November 2020 focused on employee perspectives on working in the pandemic.

### *Phase One: June 2020*

In June 2020, the researchers held online focus groups with Whistler employers. This had been their first experience conducting focus groups using Zoom to collect data, and they were pleased and somewhat relieved that it had worked well. Data collection for Phase One of the study was completed after holding four focus groups between June 22 and June 26, 2020, with a total of 28 participants. To analyse the employee data collected in these focus groups, the researchers completed a thematic analysis, in which they coded the data and highlighted the key themes, and this process revealed several pressing issues.

The data analysis indicated that the pandemic had brought several new staffing considerations for employers. The focus groups' participants had discussed several issues, including health and wellbeing, staffing, and work life balance. Health and wellbeing were a primary focus, along with the immediate need to follow provincial public health and safety protocols. Finding and retaining staff continued to be a challenge in Whistler. Prior to the pandemic, Whistler tourism employers had relied on international workers to fill their seasonal frontline roles, with many positions being filled by people on temporary visas. Now, employers had a smaller, domestic recruitment pool to draw from, and business forecasting was uncertain. With schools closed, employers shared a considerable concern they had about how parents with children would be able to continue to balance parenting and work commitments. Some staff had resigned or taken leave to focus on parenting children at home, and others were juggling work and parenting.

### *Phase Two: November 2020*

With Phase One completed, the researchers conducted three focus groups on November 23 and 24, 2020 with a total of 10 participants. The participants were employees who worked in SMEs in Whistler's tourism industry. The participants were asked to describe ways the pandemic had affected them in the workplace, and what types of support they needed in their job. As in Phase One, the researchers completed a thematic analysis to analyse the data collected in Phase Two.

## The Employee Focus Groups: Research Notes by Category

After the researchers had completed the thematic analysis, they were able to write up their notes on six categories: 1) uncertainty, 2) changes, 3) communication, 4) decision making, 5) future employment, and 6) support (Exhibit 4.2).

### *Category One: Uncertainty*

The researchers learned that the pandemic had generated multiple employee concerns broadly connected to a deep-seated feeling of uncertainty. Uncertainty was experienced in multiple ways, including financial uncertainty, the work schedule, workplace restrictions, and employees' social life. With regard to financial uncertainty, participants were concerned that their jobs might be eliminated, or they would be asked to work fewer hours. The employee research participants shared that some employers had supported them as they applied for wage subsidies. Employees also experienced uncertainty because work schedules were changed for many reasons; for example, scheduled shifts were cancelled, hours were reduced, and/or hours were increased. In addition, workplace restrictions created uncertainty about how employees should interact with customers and how they could go about their job tasks. Due to the changing nature of pandemic restrictions, plans and procedures for re-opening had been frequently revisited and changed. Employees' social lives suffered as a direct result of the workplace restrictions. Several employees shared that they missed social connection at work with their customers and co-workers, as well their interactions outside the workplace.

### *Category Two: Changes*

The researchers identified two main employee concerns relating to the workplace changes: location of their work and working conditions. Employees discussed several challenges associated with the location of their work as they moved to remote interactions and away from connecting in person with co-workers, clients, and customers. The employees had discussed the lack of boundaries, distraction, working in small spaces at home, and not meeting with their co-workers. In addition, the employees had a variety of experiences with the changing working conditions, noting the importance of having a supportive team to work with, building a common community understanding, the issues of working in sanitised environments, longer work hours, pollution, and wondering if it would be possible to return to conditions that they had pre-pandemic.

### *Category Three: Communication*

Workplace communication featured in all the discussions the researchers had with the employees. Because communication methods changed, employees were keen to provide examples of how they interacted with each other, with clients and customers, and with their employer. The three main communication aspects that the employees spoke about were communication tools, employee preferences, and what it was like working online. Employees talked about the variety of ways they communicated during the workday, and noted that there were differences in frequency, and often specific reasons for using each communication tool. Examples were given of communication that included emails, in-person, phone calls, newsletters, text, and video conferencing. In the discussions, employees' preferences were identified and included a range of technologies and techniques. Some employees missed the face-to-face meetings, while others liked emails as they allowed for reflection. In one case, an employee had used an online tool that provided a better organisational structure than that presented in texts and emails, and they thought it would be a good option for employers. Employees also gave examples of their experiences when they moved to working online and discussed the reassurance that was provided, the number of meetings they took part in, the benefits of having phone conversations, and the difference in communication styles of employers.

### Category Four: Decision Making

Because pandemic restrictions moved quickly, employers had many new situations to consider, and had to respond in a limited amount of time. This created some stressors for employees who expressed concerns about the decision-making approaches taken by some employers when there was limited consultation. However, in other cases, employees noted that they were given opportunities to be involved in the decision making, provided with ample opportunity to be part of the team, and were encouraged to take part in problem solving with their employer.

### Category Five: Future Employment

The future employment category included two themes that captured what employees had discussed, and these were precariousness of employment and new opportunities. There was discussion related to the effects of the pandemic on employment in tourism and hospitality, and the precariousness of employment during the pandemic. Tourism employment in the COVID-19 pandemic was also viewed by some as hazardous. However, some employees were affected more positively in their employment during COVID-19 with new opportunities. These opportunities related to additional training, webinars, and expanded roles in the workplace.

### Category Six: Support

Employees shared their support needs with the researchers. The researchers identified five related themes in this category which were: financial support, flexibility, mental health, relationships, and lack of support. For financial support, employees provided several examples to illustrate the range of support they had appreciated during the pandemic. Employees appreciated having flexibility in the workplace in areas such as their work hours, schedule, and sick days. Employees also raised mental health as another significant theme associated with support. Mental health was supported through counselling services and mental health days. Several participants explained that they appreciated supportive relationships in their employment. For example, when management expressed empathy, appreciation, and recognition, this was viewed as fundamental to a positive working environment. While there were many areas where employees appeared appreciative of the support provided by their employer, there were also some participants who noted that they had not had a positive experience or knew others who had felt a lack of support.

On completion of the thematic analysis and the generation of the six categories, the researchers turned to practical application, as they saw an opportunity to develop some broad recommendations that could be shared with Whistler's SME employers. The challenge ahead was to ensure that these recommendations were presented as actionable practises for employers to consider and use. The recommendations would have to be provided to Whistler Chamber employers via Zoom, so the presentation would need to be both dynamic and focused. It was important to ensure that any recommendations shared were generated from the research data analysis that they had completed.

**Discussion Questions**

1 What were the characteristics of the pandemic uncertainty that affected employees and employers?
2 What strategies would you use to improve employer to employee communication, and why would you recommend these strategies?
3 What supports could the employer adopt to help employees working at home?
4 What information is not present in the data the researchers collected that you consider pertinent in this case?

**Learning Activity: Create a Conceptual Map**

Considering the case facts, share practises to improve two-way communication between employees and employers, and be sure to link these practises to the types of workplace support employees said they needed in the pandemic. Share your suggested practises in a conceptual map on one whiteboard or PowerPoint slide. Provide a 300–400-word summary of your concept map to further explain the linkages and relationships it presents.

## Notes

1 https://www.whistlerchamber.com/almost-half-of-bc-businesses-that-are-temporarily-closed-not-confident-in-ability-to-reopen/
2 https://www.whistler.ca/about/facts-and-figures 11,854 permanent residents (2016 Canada Census) 3.48 million annual visitors (2016/17)

## References and Suggested Reading

Axe, J., Wilson-Mah, R., & Dahlquist-Axe, H. (2022). COVID-19 workplace adaptation and recovery in the resort municipality of Whistler, BC, Canada. *International Journal of Workplace Health Management 15*(3), 375–392. Available at: https://doi.org/10.1108/IJWHM-03-2021-0066

Axe, J., & Wilson-Mah, R. (2020, September). *COVID-19 adaptation and recovery: Human resource and training needs in Whistler, BC.* Final report (distributed through zero ceiling).

Cooper, C., & Hesketh, I. (Eds.). (2022). *Managing workplace health and wellbeing during a crisis: How to support your staff in difficult times.* London: Kogan Page.

## Further Reading Related to Conceptual Maps

Frisendal, T. (2012). "How to do concept mapping." In *Design thinking business analysis* (pp. 61–80). Springer Berlin Heidelberg.

Villalón, J. J., & Calvo, R. A. (2011). Concept maps as cognitive visualizations of writing assignments. *Educational Technology & Society, 14*(3), 16–27.

## Exhibits

**Exhibit 4.1** Pulse Survey Check #4 Results: Bold Plan Needed to Help Businesses Recover, July 16, 2020

The Whistler Chamber and the BC Chamber of Commerce have collaborated once again to collect important data from Whistler's businesses on the effects Covid-19 continues to have. The Whistler Chamber continues to share this data with all levels of government to ensure your voice is heard and the right amount of support is available to help you get back on your feet as quickly as possible.

### Provincial Overview

While British Columbia has entered Phase Three of its Restart Plan, two-thirds (65 percent) of businesses surveyed are using some form of government support. Businesses expect a substantial "second wave" of negative impacts should these programs expire too quickly.

Only about three-in-ten businesses (28 percent) on government support expect to return to normal once the programs end. Of the remainder, 32 percent expect to reduce employee hours, 27 percent expect to lay-off or terminate employees, and 24 percent anticipate taking on debt. One-in-ten will have to close either temporarily or permanently.

The findings are the results of a survey of 1,401 member-businesses of the BC Chamber of Commerce, Greater Vancouver Board of Trade, Business Council of British Columbia, and partners including the Whistler Chamber of Commerce, with the Mustel Group's assistance. This survey is the fourth in a series of pulse checks using the BCMindReader.com platform.

As the BC government works on its $1.5 billion recovery plan, bold vision will be required to help businesses survive in the short term and the economy to be competitive and resilient in the future. However, businesses are not particularly confident that the recovery plan will help their business succeed or survive. Only 16 percent are confident, compared to 47 percent that are not confident.

Businesses say the most important components of the recovery plan are providing payroll or wage supports and reducing fees. Cutting red tape, creating better investment conditions, direct cash flow support, and making regulations more efficient are other notable suggestions.

### Whistler Findings

Thank you to those who completed the 4th Pulse Check survey. Here are the results from the Whistler business community:

#### *Impact on Business*

27 percent have seen a 75–100 percent drop in sales over the past two weeks, while 25 percent have seen between 50 and 74 percent

43 percent have seen up to 20 percent of their normal revenue in the last 30 days, while only 18 percent have seen between 20 and 39 percent

38 percent felt the cost of implementing measures to adhere to health and safety requirements was expensive to very expensive

43 percent of businesses have one to five positions unfilled

***BC Government Recovery Plan and Support***

31 percent would like to see this plan released ASAP while 50 percent are in favor of waiting until full consultation has been conducted

45 percent are not particularly confident in the recovery plan once it is launched

87 percent of Whistler businesses are using government support programs:

62 percent – CEWS

28 percent – CECRA

26 percent – Tax deferrals

CEBA – 26 percent

Here are the top three most important component of any recovery/building plan. Here is what you said

Providing payroll/wage support – 65 percent

Reducing taxes/fee – 39 percent

Support with direct cash flow – 39 percent

Workplace Changes

***Top Barriers to Getting Employees Back to Work***

28 percent say the health/safety concerns in the workplace are a top barrier to getting employees back to work

27 percent say that as a result of social distancing requirements, it limits the number of employees allowed in the workplace

53 percent are unsure what they will do when the temporary layoff period ends at the end of August

14 percent are planning to bring back all laid off employees

11 percent will pay severance to all laid off employees

What additional Government support/programs would be most helpful to your Biz during recovery? Here is what you said:

63 percent – provide more wage support

44 percent – provide more effective rent relief

39 percent – provide more effective cash flow relief

38 percent – provide greater tax relief

"Policy-makers and politicians must stay sensitive to how vulnerable BC businesses are today. Entrepreneurs are waking up to the reality that their new operating environment is more costly and fraught with risk. A bold economic recovery plan that helps small businesses compete is a non-negotiable for a prosperous BC – and when small businesses thrive so do communities and people. Governments must keep focussed on delivering their recovery plans swiftly." Val Litwin, President & CEO, BC Chamber of Commerce

Source: Whistler pulse check, july 16, 2020. https://www.whistlerchamber.com/pulse-check-4-results-bold-plan-needed-to-help-businesses-survive/ with permission.

**Exhibit 4.2** Six Categories Generated by Thematic Analysis of Focus Groups with Quotations from Whistler SME Employee Focus Group Participants (November 2020)

1 **UNCERTAINTY**

a Financial

"She ensured that we got wage subsidies for the company and that sort of thing so then we can eat you know, so that we can keep our core staff working" (FG1)

b Work Schedules

"I've definitely taken on more than I was hired to do" (FG3)

"... everything's just kind of up in the air so it's like, it's hard to make solid decisions right now" (FG3)

c Workplace Restrictions

"... .all the procedures have affected us a lot ... work is not as enjoyable" (FG1)

"You make a plan and then, then you find out that okay actually that's not what we're going to be able to do because of restrictions ... it felt like sometimes you were doing work that didn't go anywhere" (FG3)

d Social Lives

"... it's kind of weird for me because I don't really thrive in this virtual world we are living in right now" (FG2)

"... when you're 20 years old, away from home, you came here to party and go on adventures and now you're stuck at home away from your family" (FG2)

2 **CHANGE**

a Location of Their Work

"Not having that boundary ... I am having challenges into like separating my personal and then my work time already and because of the number of factors like you would also be distracted from time to time working from home, like, 'Oh, I need to do something [with] my laundry'" (FG1)

"Having a small space working in your kitchen counter or in one, one meter wide table in one corner of the house is proving to be challenging in the long run." (FG1)

"Now that I can do some of that work online it's almost created a little bit more time." (FG1)

"I like don't really thrive in this like virtual world that we're kind of living in right now." (FG2)

"I haven't seen any of my coworkers in person for a very long time." (FG3)

b Working Conditions

"I have a great team to kind of help me navigate how things are supposed to look, or how things usually are versus kind of how they are now and what we have to limit, or change, or just adapt." (FG1)

"People love to socialize, but I'm very cautious because you know I have asthma so I'm at risk for some of those more respiratory issues. And I was wearing masks ... but like not all my coworkers felt the same." (FG2)

"These anti mask protesters and so you have a specific guideline for that protocol to follow ... it would still be useful for people in the community not just in one employer or organization to ... just identify it as black or white. So it would be easier for the community to be able to have a common understanding of everything." (FG1)

"Going from you know working in a super relaxed cafe to working in just a sanitized bubble." (FG2)

"Is it ever going to go back to what it was like?" (FG2)

"How much more pollution are we going to put out there on top of what we're already doing?" (FG2)

"My days were full because I would go and spend an hour and a half, with one family then half an hour, travel, and then sanitation time. And then another family would come in." (FG3)

"I would even say there's right like currently there's so many things that are changing it's almost too much." (FG3)

3 **COMMUNICATION**

a Communication Tools

"Facetime meetings, emails, phone calls." (FG1)

"Now we have to do an internal communication newsletter." (FG1)

"We were meeting, physically distant, the senior management team there's about seven of us so we were meeting in our large circle outside." (FG1)

"Emails, if it's an emergency phone call if it's a text message, any anything, any way we can reach each other because things change quickly. So, it's, it's mostly that, lots of meetings." (FG2)

"We had at least one zoom meeting face to face, online per day, or per week, sorry, sometimes more than that. And then, texts texts for sure an email for sure as well." (FG3)

b Employees Preferences

"Definitely missing the in-person meetings with our team." (FG1)

"A meeting every time before we started work was really useful ... I really value emails like some people don't prefer them personally, but I like them, you just give me the information, let me read, let me analyze it myself." (FG2)

"The moral support, and the team meetings every week do help they're kind of like a little bit of an inconvenience and stuff like that but it does help like see people's faces and be like, oh, we're not just like text on a screen." (FG2)

"I've used different apps like Slack, and that's the one I've used where everything when you're communicating it's very it's in a specific channel so you can go back and look at what was there, where with email and with text, it's so lost ... so many emails I don't know where it is. I would say just specifically for my organization like adopting a tool like that would make communication a lot better." (FG3)

c Working Online

"My employer is very communicative and it's great – she's always researching the new information and ensuring our team is on board with changes and reassuring us in terms of our business moving forward." (FG1)

"I don't think I've ever participated in so many meetings in my life ... I think a lot of us had Zoom fatigue ... I had to get new glasses actually." (FG1)

"I think she felt that it was really inundating to go through the emails. And so she have done like an over the phone conversation one on one." (FG1)

"It was interesting for me to see how different employers would. For example, one would maybe just forward all the new health regulations and I would be just like see here's this attached, take a look at that, acknowledge that you've read this, and then another employer would send it but then also kind of summarize it and distill it and how it directly relates to the work." (FG1)

4 **DECISION MAKING**

"[Decisions were about] how to keep the safe place, how to keep customers safe, how to make, you know, make sure that everyone is respecting the rules, things like disinfecting the entire cafe, every hour right, customer side, our side. So this is all decision making. And, yeah, a lot, a lot of weird things that we've never had to do before." (FG2)

"Our manager will come to us and ask, how do you guys feel about this like how do you think that will work – and really values our input so I really respect that. COVID or not I think that's a really great thing and I'm happy to be a part of a space like this." (FG1)

"I'm definitely involved [in the decision-making process], we're like right in the mix together, for sure." (FG2)

"As the pandemic was going on we were creating our return to sport plan and creating the protocols and policies that we would need to use when we wanted to return to sport and they really really used the frontline staff who are going to be the ones, implementing these protocols and policies with athletes and volunteers ... It was very much a team effort and felt very included in that." (FG3)

5 **FUTURE EMPLOYMENT**

a Precariousness of Employment

"Now, a lot more dangerous and just with like, you know COVID being a factor, and it's not essential." (FG2)

"It made me realize how precarious my employment situation was, and then the biggest thing that came out of it ... I need to find a change ... it's just not sustainable for the life I want to live." (FG2)

"I am going back to school to just completely change careers." (FG2)

b New Opportunities

"I definitely think a lot of the skills that I've used over the last few months are super transferable to other organizations." (FG2)

"I've expanded what my position actually is so I'm into different courses now." (FG3)

6 **SUPPORT**

a Financial Support

"Funding was given for online conferences." (FG1)

"Small monetary support, for example reimbursing what they have used up on personal equipment." (FG1)

"We got wage subsidies for the company and that sort of thing so then we can eat, you know, so that we can keep our core staff working." (FG1)

"She's the research knowledge powerhouse so she would make sure that we all fully understood, sort of what we had access [to]." (FG1)

"Making sure they know about our EAP program and using their benefits." (FG1) b Flexibility

"I'm a single parent so when the schools were closed I was able to adjust my schedule to help my son with his online schooling, extra sick/mental health days." (FG1)

"It is such a drastic difference in regards to the reaction from employers/managers in the daily navigating of the pandemic. For example, not feeling guilty or ashamed if you are potentially experiencing symptoms or unsure if you should come into work or not. It has been very positive for me here – they care and are supportive rather than penalize you for things beyond your control. Good management makes a huge difference in the workplace especially during these uncharted times." (FG1)

c Mental Health

"Our team gets to meet with like a counselor and just kind of go over things either related to COVID or how we're feeling or how we're feeling in relation to our roles and things that come up ... having that support and understanding all around unconditionally has been really welcoming and just makes it a positive experience." (FG1)

"I'm just supporting them that way and again as well with mental health days and 100% there's more of those going around." (FG1)

"When you're 20 years old, away from home, you came here to party and go on adventures and now you stuck at home away from your family during a pandemic, right, so lots of mental health support." (FG2)

d Relationships

"[The employer is] aware of these things and where everyone's coming from and everyone's experiencing this, but it's through a different lens; it's very very clear that you don't know what has happened to someone else earlier in the day ... just approaching everyone with empathy and compassion." (FG1)

"Lots of presence, you know if there's any questions I know that all the time I can talk to my manager and she'll be there for me and lots of support, and she's just very available which is really nice." (FG2)

"[It] was very important for us to use the staff recognition and appreciation line in our budget; that was something that was, you know, just buying doughnuts and coffee like I'm telling you these little things, we can't go out for drinks anymore after work, and all these little things and giving them grocery gift certificates." (FG1)

e Lack of Support

"My sister has so much anxiety ... our experiences during this whole thing have been so drastically different ... it's really not in her control or not her fault but she's having really a much harder time with it. So I just think that shows the difference of having a supportive team and having people on your side rather than literally being penalized or being, you know, taken off the schedule or something if you have had to isolate." (FG1)

"I didn't really receive a lot of support from any of my employers." (FG2)

"I was working about 16–17 kilometers north of where I lived. And, to get to work, I would have to catch a bus and then walk three kilometers along the highway. And originally there was transportation in place but then they like, stop doing that, so it took me like I almost got to work like an hour early because that was when the last bus." (FG2)

Source: Anonymized data set from the case authors.

# PART 2

# Sustainable Tourism in Context

The cases focus on a range of approaches taken to contribute to a sustainable path for tourism development and operations in different contexts.

DOI: 10.4324/9781003280040-8

# CASE 5

## RURAL TOURISM GROWTH IN GHALEGAUN, NEPAL

*Himal Poudel, Brian White, and Charles Krusekopf*

**Synopsis**

On June 10, 2018, in peak tourist season in the village of Ghalegaun in Gandaki Province in Western Nepal, Prem Bahadur Ghale, the local tourism leader received a frantic call from the secretary of the local Tourism Management Committee (TMC). A large group of domestic tourists, which also included some VIPs, had just arrived in front of the village requesting overnight accommodation. The homestays in the village were all fully occupied, and the personnel stationed at the village gate tourist entry point were having difficulties handling the situation. Prem Bahadur Ghale was concerned that travellers with unconfirmed reservations had no place to stay, and this was the second incident that week.

Prem Bahadur was excited about the growing number of tourists coming to the province. There was a growing demand for tourist accommodation, and tourists had started to express a desire for other types of accommodation and a better quality of service. Prem Bahadur knew that his small village had reached capacity. Due to the limited homestays in Ghalegaun, tourists had been transferred to nearby Bhujung village. He knew that there was no easy solution to the problem, and he was also concerned that other tourism options would develop in other villages and his village might be left behind. In his mind, there was work ahead to bring local villagers together to come up with a more permanent solution.

### Before Tourism in Ghalegaun

Before tourism started in 2000, no one outside Nepal knew about Ghalegaun, and the village was a poor and remote rural village. Situated at an altitude of 2,100 meters above sea level in the Lamjung district of the Mid-Western region of Nepal, the village had no roads and was inaccessible. To reach Ghalegaun, people had to walk a day from Besisahar,

DOI: 10.4324/9781003280040-9

the nearest city and also headquarter of Lamjung (Exhibit 5.1). The lifeline for Ghalegaun was connected, both administratively and economically, by a system of trails to Besisahar. Locals commuted every day to Besisahar for trade and household groceries, and for education, health, and public administration. Groceries were fetched using porters by horseback. There was no electricity in the village. People relied on kerosene lamps and lamps made from pine (dhoopisalla). A few houses that could afford more brought and installed small capacity solar panels and lamps from Besisahar or Pokhara.

Although situated only 108 km northwest of Kathmandu, Ghalegaun had struggled with basic development. Most of the village people were illiterate. There was a persistently high school dropout rate, and very few villagers graduated from high school. Only a few could afford to send their sons and daughters for higher education in big cities such as Besisahar, Pokhara, or Kathmandu. There were no jobs in the village, and most people relied on sustenance farming and animal rearing. There was an increasing trend of migration of adults to big cities and abroad for an improved livelihood. There was only a primary health post in the village that lacked skilled doctors and nurses. People had a very poor sense of sanitation and hygiene, and only a handful of houses had toilets. There was no water line system in the village, and people had to take turns to fetch daily water, including drinking water, from a nearby waterspout.

## Prem Bahadur Leads Tourism Development and Homestays

Tourism started in Ghalegaun when trekkers in the region heard about Ghalegaun during their layover at Besisahar, and a few of them decided to take a different route. Trekkers navigating the Annapurna region in the summer of 2000 were the early guests to the first eight homestays.

Tourism development first began to increase in 2011 through the hard work of the villagers under the direction of Prem Bahadur Ghale. Born and raised in Ghalegaun, Prem Bahadur was determined to improve the economic opportunities and living conditions of the villagers in Ghalegaun through tourism development. He had been to places like Pokhara and Sirubari and seen tourism there firsthand. He was also aware that his village was in the Annapurna Conservation Area Project (ACAP), a region where several famous trekking routes were located, including the one to Annapurna base camp. He was convinced that his village had aspects that would make it a great destination for both foreign trekkers in the region and domestic tourists looking for a getaway. He had a vision for his village that other residents couldn't imagine. The challenge he faced was to conceive a concept for tourism development and convince his fellow villagers to support and help implement the concept.

Prem Bahadur was first introduced to the concept of homestays and rural tourism during his visit to Sirubari, one of the first villages in Nepal that had adopted rural village tourism, with a focus on homestays. Sirubari was regarded as a model village in all hilly Nepal, and every pretty village in the hills aspired to be like Sirubari. Prem Bahadur had seen the success Sirubari had attracting visitors, and he became convinced that Ghalegun could follow a similar path. Prem Bahadur recalled:

> I felt that Ghalegaun was way prettier than Sirubari and we had more to offer to tourists. Ghalegaun has a beautifully patterned settlement, panoramic view of the mountains, blessed nature, and rich culture. It is the perfect mountain village. What more did you need to attract tourists? I was convinced that we could attract loads of tourists.

Prem Bahadur and the villagers reviewed every nook and corner of Ghalegaun and considered every detail of their culture and livelihood. They jointly pondered upon every potentiality and barrier to tourism development. The villagers formed a Tourism Management Committee (TMC) with nine members for tourism planning, administration, and advocacy. Prem Bahadur was unanimously elected the chairperson of the committee. Prem Bahadur knew about the village tourism program in the Tourism Policy of Nepal, established in 1995. The government of Nepal later introduced Homestay Operating Guidelines in 2011, and these guidelines were adopted by Ghalegaun. The committee was engaged in designing tourism products and services that they would serve and sell. They decided to go with the tried and tested homestay model that villagers could invest in without being trapped in a big line of debt. The foods served to guests would be the same food that households would normally eat, traditional Gurung food – they were operating rural tourism after all. The villagers were all motivated, and they all got together toward a common goal. Their vision, as stated in the preamble of the RTDC, was "to develop a prosperous village through tourism promotion." Six months later, rural tourism with its own geographical and cultural uniqueness was initiated in Ghalegaun.

By 2018, tourism had grown, and Ghalegaun was one of the largest homestay villages in Nepal with over 50 homestays (Exhibit 5.2). Ghalegaun was among the most coveted places to visit in western Nepal, recognised for pristine nature and scenic grandeur and the hospitality of traditional Ghale culture.

## Changes and Transitions – The Path to Rural Tourism

The early days of tourism were very exciting for the villagers as they were all experiencing an entirely different way of thinking that reflected their aim to be a rural tourism village. Most of the marketing was done via villagers' personal connections with tourism operators based in Kathmandu, Pokhara, and Besisahar. An art festival and a cultural festival also helped GhaleGuan to become more known for tourism in Nepal. Eight houses invested in building or maintaining one extra room to accommodate a maximum of two guests. The average investment by each household was NPR. 10000 ($78 USD), and additional financial support was provided by the Annapurna Conservation Area Project (ACAP). Prem Bahadur was among the initial investors. A mere 62 tourists visited Ghalegaun in the first year, generating average revenue of about NPR. 3000. All the tourists visiting Ghalegaun in the first year were domestic tourists. By the end of the first year, four more houses had invested in homestays. Forty people were directly involved in tourism. Despite the lack of infrastructure, tourism slowly started to grow.

Tourism was very basic in the early days. Tired tourists reaching Ghalegaun after an entire day of hiking from Besisahar, were traditionally welcomed by the newly formed mother's group (AamaSamuha). They were served local foods, and at night all villagers and tourists enjoyed the cultural show filled with traditional songs and dances. Dim solar lights and kerosene lamps lit the homestays and the newly built cultural hall in the centre of the village. Tourists were provided with battery-powered torch lights so that they could find their way at night to toilets located a short walk from the house.

The installation of toilets in a rural village inhabited by poor traditional people was a new development. "If it wasn't for tourism, the villagers would never have built toilets," claimed Prem Bahadur. He had to spend a lot of his time persuading people to consider changes to their way of life, including building toilets. Five years after tourism development in 2005, all the houses had built toilets, and the village was declared an open defecation-free zone. Next, the villagers had to lobby the district administrative offices a countless number of times asking them for roads. "Villagers were worshipping the first vehicles that reached the village. The drivers were well-fed" recalled Prem Bahadur when he remembered the early days after the road was finally opened in 2008, eight years after the first homestay began operation. After years of perseverance, in 2011, the locally produced hydroelectricity finally lit the village. Ghalegaun was finally flying high in its desire for prosperity, and tourism was its sail.

## Changing Tourist Demand

Between 2000 and 2010 the number of homestays increased almost threefold to 33 (Exhibit 5.3). The average investment of each household now stood at NPR. 30,000. ACAP was still supporting the villagers financially. The number of tourists averaged out annually at 15,000, among which the largest chunk of visitors was domestic tourists at 83%. The number of organised parties visiting Ghalegaun was increasing annually as well with the decade-end figure standing at 75%. By now, at least 150 people were directly involved in tourism. Many side businesses started to pop up and included one community tea farm, one sheep farm and one local souvenir shop. Three more gift shops and one restaurant were open by 2010. The monthly average revenue from tourism in this period fluctuated between NPR. 10000 and 25000 – depending on months within and outside the tourism season.

Only ten years after the first homestays were opened in 2000, Ghalegaun was declared the number one model village by the South Asian Association for Regional Cooperation (SAARC). The village was all set to be declared the "Happiest Village" in all of Nepal. The President of Nepal herself was expected to visit Ghalegaun on the day of the declaration. All these accolades topped with two decades of tourism had increased the popularity of Ghalegaun among domestic tourists in Nepal. Ghalegaun was starting to witness large business groups from banks and institutions, and groups of college students ranging in size from four to 50.

With the increase in number and types of visitors came an increase in types of demands. Many tourists came in groups, especially young people, and they wanted to stay together. They didn't like to be separated into smaller groups to be accommodated in different houses. If groups wanted to stick together, there was no way any house could accommodate them. Homestay hosts were also finding it difficult to provide for large groups of guests. The catering needs of guests kept the hosts awake late into the night. The situation was like nothing imagined during the initial tourism planning and designing done two decades ago. There was an increasing risk that tourism in the village of Ghalegaun might deviate away from its original approach of rural tourism. However, Prem Bahadur and the villagers did not want to lose any business by turning away any guest wanting to visit their beautiful village.

With only a few months left in the tourism season this year, Prem Bahadur was feeling the pressure to address capacity issues for the season next year. He was the one the villagers looked up to for a reasonable solution. As far as he could see, no obvious options were viable anymore: all interested houses were already operating homestays; uninterested houses couldn't be forced, and all the homestays were operating at full capacity. How should Prem Bahadur proceed to guide and support sustainable rural tourism development in Ghalegaun?

## Discussion Questions

1 What are the challenges for developing rural tourism based on the narrative of the given case?
2 What are the benefits and key steps for developing rural tourism in the case, and what weaknesses can you identify?
3 What are the strengths and weaknesses of Ghalegaun in developing and sustaining tourism?
4 What are the key steps to consider when planning for sustainable rural tourism growth?
5 What are the other options and alternatives for improving business that the villagers might consider?

## Learning Activity: Application of successful community-based tourism (CBT) for rural destinations

Nair, V., & Hamzah, A. (2015). Successful community-based tourism approaches for rural destinations: The Asia Pacific experience. *Worldwide Hospitality and Tourism Themes*, *7*(5), 429–439. doi: 10.1108/WHATT-06-2015-0023

This paper recommends nine steps for developing and sustaining community-based tourism (CBT). These nine steps are divided into two sections – developing CBT and sustaining CBT. The first four steps relate to starting and developing CBT initiatives, which are useful for projects and sites that are embarking on CBT. The subsequent five steps are meant to address the sustainability of CBT projects, which are more appropriate for mature CBT projects that are gradually moving up the value chain. For each step, a list of actions are recommended to guide the development of CBT.

Apply the nine-step model of developing and sustaining CBT (Nair & Hamzah, 2015, p 433).

Review the steps for *developing CBT initiatives*. The steps are *Step 1: Assess community needs and readiness for tourism; Step 2: Educate and prepare the community for tourism; Step 3: Identify and establish a leadership team/local champion;*and *Step 4: Prepare and develop community organisation.*

For each of the four steps, review the case, and identify where each step applies in the case. Then create a plan for each respective step for Ghalegaun based on the case.

Review the steps for *sustaining* CBT initiatives. The steps are *Step 5: Develop partnerships; Step 6: Adopt an integrated approach; Step 7: Plan and design a quality product; Step 8: Identify market demand and develop a marketing strategy;* and *Step 9: implement and monitor performance*

For each of the four steps, review the case, and identify where each step applies in the case. Then create a plan for each the respective step for Ghalegaun based on the case.

On completion of this analysis consider the following questions:

1 Which step do you think Ghalegaun is currently at?
2 What are the general challenges for rural tourism at each of the nine steps?
3 What strengths and/or weaknesses can you identify for each step for Ghalegaun?

## References and Suggested Reading

Acharya, B. P., & Halpenny, E. A. (2013). Homestays as an alternative tourism product for sustainable community development: A case study of women-managed tourism product in rural Nepal. *Tourism Planning & Development, 10*(4), 367–367. Available at: https://doi.org/10.1080/21568316.2013.779313

Across Himalaya Tours and Treks. P. Ltd. (n.d.). Available at: https://www.acrosshimalaya.com/nepal/village/Ghalegaun-village-tour.html

Himalya Guide. (n.d.). Available at: https://himalayaguidenepal.com/ghale-gaunhomestay-trek/

Nair, V., & Hamzah, A. (2015). Successful community-based tourism approaches for rural destinations: The Asia Pacific experience. *Worldwide Hospitality and Tourism Themes, 7*(5), 429–439. doi: 10.1108/WHATT-06-2015-0023

## Exhibits

### Exhibit 5.1 Map of Ghalegaun

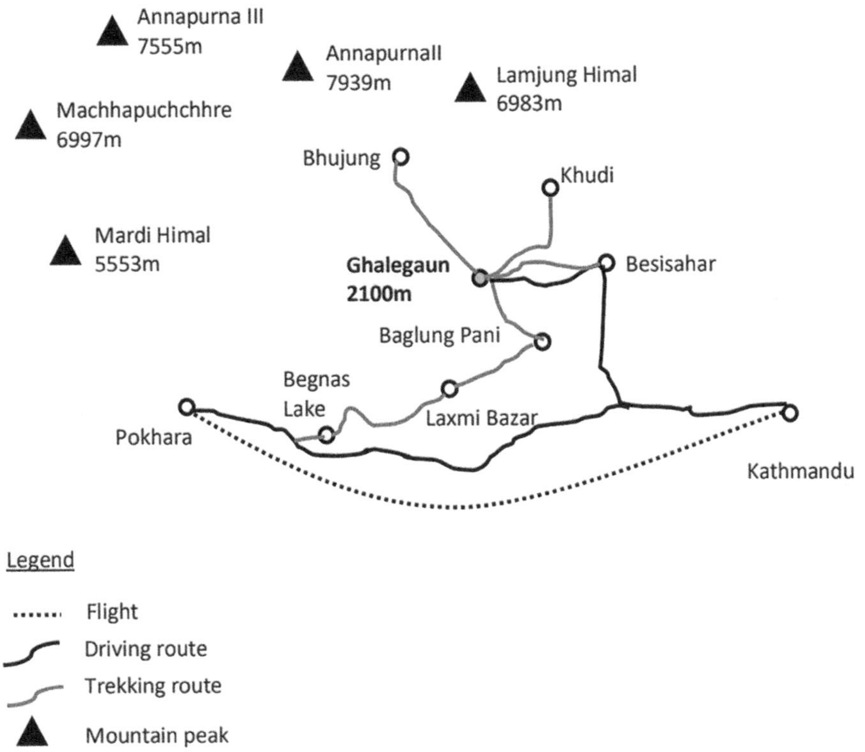


Source: Location Map of Ghalegaun prepared by the authors.

**Exhibit 5.2** Photograph of Ghalegaun

Source: Across Himalaya tours and treks. P. Ltd. n.d., https://www.acrosshimalaya.com/nepal/village/Ghalegaun-village-tour.html.

**Exhibit 5.3** Tourism Statistics for Ghalegaun

| Tourism Statistics for Ghalegaun | 2000 | 2010 |
|---|---|---|
| Total number of houses in Ghalegaun | 115 | 121 |
| Number of homestays | 12 | 33 |
| Number of rooms | 12 | 66 |
| Total Guest Catering Capacity per night | 24 | 200 |
| Average no. of rooms per homestay (for guests) | 1 | 2 |
| Average Guests Capacity per homestay per night | 2 | 4 |
| Package Price per night* | NPR 650 | NPR 950 |
| Average Investment per household | NPR 10,000 +Support by ACAP and village municipality | NPR 30,000 |
| Average revenue per household (monthly) | NPR 3,000 | NPR 10,000-25,000 |
| Average number of people involved in running homestay per household | 2 | 3 |
| Number of people directly involved in tourism | 40 | 150 |
| No. of tourists (domestic) | 62 | 10520 |
| % of organised tourist parties | Not available | 75% |
| Number of tourists (international) | Not available | 349 |
| % of free individual tourists | Not available | 25% |

Source: Table authors' own. Data from ACAP, Unit conservation office, Bhujung; ACAP check post and information center, Ghalegaun; Village tourism development committee, Ghalegaun.

*Package Includes: Bed, Breakfast, Lunch, and Dinner.

# CASE 6

## A SUSTAINABLE TOURISM PLAN AND REBRAND FOR LAGOS, NIGERIA

*Oluwafisayo Olayinka-Bello and Rebecca Wilson-Mah*

**Synopsis**

On April 2, 2021, Adun Okupe, CEO of Red Clay Advisory, and her team were appointed to develop and translate the Lagos State Tourism Master Plan (LSTMP) into a simplified tourism plan. Tourism stakeholders had not been optimally supported to implement the previous LSTMP because the document was extensive and not easy to implement. The primary constraints for Red Clay Advisory for the project were the six-week timeline and tourism stakeholders' need for a proper understanding of the tourism plan. The international media had emphasised Nigeria's shortcomings, and this had affected the country's reputation as an unsafe place for tourists and investors.

On April 2, 2021, Adunola Okupe was honoured when her team at Red Clay Advisory was appointed by the Commissioner for Lagos State Ministry of Culture, Arts and Tourism to develop and translate the Lagos State Tourism Master Plan (LSTMP) into a simplified tourism plan for the tourism industry. Founded by Okupe in 2017, Red Clay Advisory specialises in tourism consultancy projects in Africa. The project timeline was tight, with only six weeks assigned for the project completion. Okupe aimed to take the current 400-page LSTMP document and distil it into approximately 35 pages. Okupe was concerned about the tight timeframe and the scope of the work ahead that the team had broadly organised into a six-week timeline in a quick list early that day (Exhibit 6.1).

Tourism stakeholders had not been optimally supported to implement the previous LSTMP because the document was extensive and not easy to action. Okupe and her team were at the start of their six-week timeline. With a six-week timeline, there was work to do practically and tactically to articulate the plan for Lagos' tourism industry. The team needed to complete a tourism plan for Lagos with an associated direction for a destination rebrand

DOI: 10.4324/9781003280040-10

while ensuring stakeholder engagement and buy-in. A key project goal was to establish practical strategies to attract new international tourists and enhance the experience of domestic and existing international tourists. The team also wanted to make sustainability a forefront consideration regarding their long-term thinking – socially, environmentally, and economically. In a discussion, Okupe said, "*It is not just about climate change; it is also about making sure that the people working in the industry have a good living.*"

## Adunola Okupe

Before her appointment to the project, Adunola Okupe had volunteered to work on a few projects with the Commissioner for the Lagos State Ministry of Culture, Arts, and Tourism. Okupe had completed distinguished work for the Ministry, which contributed to the Commissioner's decision to appoint this project to Okupe and her team at Red Clay Advisory. With over 15 years in the travel and tourism industry, Okupe was a researcher and economist with a PhD in strategic leadership in the Tourism Industry from the University of Surrey. Okupe was also a qualified chartered accountant with the Institute of Chartered Accountants of Scotland. She had a BSc in economics from Keele University (2006), and an MSc in development studies from the School of Oriental African Studies (SOAS) University of London (2010). When working with complex teams and government agencies, she drew knowledge from her PhD in emotional intelligence, social intelligence, and behavioural psychology. Okupe liked working with people and had a passion for organising people and projects. She realised she enjoyed connecting with people and "*making sure everyone was on the same page.*" The impetus for completing a master's degree in development studies was because she saw tourism as an opportunity for sustainable development. In 2010 she worked with The World Travel & Tourism Council (WTTC) as a policy and research analyst, after which she started consulting in Africa, in 2011, on hospitality and tourism projects. Okupe's consulting included work for tourism boards in Tanzania, Nigeria, Liberia, Cote D'Ivoire, and Ghana.

## Red Clay Advisory

In 2017, Okupe founded Red Clay Advisory to harness the potential of sustainable tourism in West Africa by working with government bodies to develop and translate tourism master plans. Furthermore, she provided tourism education to improve the tourism skills and capabilities of tourism stakeholders in West Africa. The name of her company was derived from the clay soil she saw in her travels through Nigeria and West Africa. The clay soil could be moulded into any object you wanted and was transformative and durable. Okupe likened this to her desire to see tourism in Nigeria moulded and developed to shape people's lives positively through the services delivered at Red Clay. The Red Clay Advisory team included Okupe, as the lead consultant, research analysts, and a research manager.

## Tourism in Nigeria and the Image Crisis

Okupe made it a priority to share Nigeria's tourism potential with the international community. She highlighted Nigeria's rich opportunity for ecotourism with waterfalls, mountains, natural landscapes, beaches, and river deltas. Nigeria had historical sites, had the world's second-largest film industry, and had pioneered a unique music genre called Afrobeat[1].

Despite these desirable natural resources, Nigeria's image stemmed from the colonial period and the first military coup d'etat in 1966[2]. In addition, vices like corruption, armed robbery, militancy, oil bunkering, human trafficking, election rigging, kidnapping, bombing, and more had tainted Nigeria's image. They had affected international tourist arrivals due to poor perception (Exhibits 6.2 and 6.3). The international media emphasised Nigeria's shortcomings, and this tarnished the country's reputation, thereby painting the country as an unsafe place for tourists and investors[3].

Okupe identified that there was a lot to do to improve tourism in Nigeria, but there was also a lack of a concerted approach to start doing what was needed. Okupe expressed ideas in a conversation with a member of the Red Clay Advisory team and said:

> A more cohesive collaboration is needed in Nigeria's tourism industry for effective impact. So much has happened already; there is a sense of travel in Nigeria's domestic tourism. However, unless there is a wider ecosystem change in transportation, accessibility, security, information, attraction upgrade and development, it will limit the impact of the stakeholders in the industry. For the change of this scale to happen, investors and the warm embrace or collaborative effort of the public and private sectors needs to happen, and we are not there yet. Once Nigeria starts having people that understand tourism's allied services and the industries and how it connects in a real distinct way, Nigeria can then start to approach tourism development more seriously.

## Tourism in Lagos

Lagos was a megacity, built on 365,861 hectares of land (Exhibit 6.3), with over 22 million residents. A coastal city, Lagos state had 12 beaches and over 18 private beach resorts. Lagos was formerly known as the capital of Nigeria, a country with 36 states. With this history, Lagos became Nigeria's commercial and cultural capital despite the change of the capital state to Abuja in 1991. This reputation had brought in business tourists in previous years, who visited Lagos for a short period and left within a few days without being involved in any tourist activity. In 2013, Lagos had 1.25 million international tourist arrivals; in 2014, it had 1.3 million; three years later, it had 1.39 million international tourists[4]. As of 2019, the total visitor spend was US$3.4 billion. Okupe believed this indicated the high earning potential in tourism if tourism was managed and marketed effectively. It was estimated that 60–80% of tourists were business tourists[5].

These factors contributed to Lagos as a centre of business activities in West Africa. Okupe understood that Lagos' primary tourist market was business tourists, who needed to be captured in future branding activities. Okupe had recently stated:

> Some of the tourism products Lagos has includes over 20 million residents, an aquatic environment, slave route history, Afro-Brazilian heritage, architecture, entertainment heritage, Nollywood (Nigeria's movie industry), the creative industries, and art theatre.

Rich in cultural heritage, Lagos held monuments that were significant for Nigeria's religious heritage and slavery heritage. Nigeria's movie industry, Nollywood, was led by the film industry in Lagos.

## Lagos State Tourism Master Plan Project

Okupe and her team had six weeks to create a simplified version of the existing LSTMP document. This work would include an in-depth review of the existing masterplan, liaising with stakeholder groups and creating new practical strategies to attract international tourists and enhance the experience of the domestic, business, and leisure tourists already existing in the state. "*A master plan is a living document, not a static document,*" Okupe said. The new simplified master plan was intended to show that Lagos State was ready for investment and private sector engagement. It also needed to give a sense of discovery to tourists. One early clear solution that Okupe pointed out to the team was the potential use of waterways and the government's partnership with water taxis, private yachts, and boat companies to create a route for tourists to explore Lagos. She believed this would help aid public-private partnership in Lagos. Okupe knew there would be a lot of intense work ahead for this to happen.

One key goal of the project was to imbibe the spirit of tourism so that the stakeholders got connected to a plan for the future. Okupe stated that "*the master plan is not meant to be a government document alone; it should encompass the stakeholder's and policymakers' perception and challenges.*" Okupe shared with her team that the "*masterplan should be relevant and tailored to the needs of the stakeholders in such a way that they can connect with and see themselves as being part of its implementation.*" Since Lagos was the country's economic and financial nerve centre, one of the goals they planned to consider was how to enhance the experience of business tourists in the state, and innovative ways to treasure, preserve, and conserve the existing heritage.

Okupe believed it was important to establish some pillars to guide communication, development, and consultation for Lagos' tourism plan. Despite the challenges envisaged on the project, Okupe found that "*when there is a will, there is a way.*" A tourism strategist and Nigerian, she relied on her experience to deliver on the project in such little time, along with the help of her team. A challenge posed for this consulting project was bureaucracy from the government and the different perspectives from tourism associations who often represented conflicting views on priorities.

## Lagos State Brand Analysis

Okupe firmly believed that the Lagos State brand was confusing and that different marketing materials lacked cohesion and had conflicting brand messaging. She believed that a re-brand was necessary and aimed to include recommendations for this in the project. She expected the project would determine ways to project a better brand for Lagos and enhance the tourist experience. Lagosians were known to have the "can do" spirit, and Okupe wondered how this could be reflected in a new slogan for Lagos state as her team started to consider how to strategise Lagos state's re-branding. The existing Lagos brand seemed to be noisy, confusing, and not relaxing.

A brand analysis conducted by Okupe and her team had shown that tourists who came to Lagos did not know places to explore in Lagos by themselves; they usually needed the help of a friend or colleague. The analysis also pointed out that Lagos was beginning to be seen as a strict place with a lot of enforcement; it also seemed that Lagosians were becoming more isolated, and the need for the focus on community connection arose. Okupe commented:

> To encourage the community connection, we need to include Lagosians in the video as part of the narrative, not just the tourism product. We need to showcase the people as part of the tourism ecosystem. Most tourists are here for business, to visit friends and relatives, for parties or to attend ceremonies. We need to be able to show that Lagos is safe, interesting and, more importantly, show that there are different things to do in Lagos. So that when business tourists are done with meetings, they look forward to places to visit instead of leaving Lagos. There is little information online regarding our attractions and things to do in Lagos. One solution to this is creating an online portal to find tour guides that are registered and accredited to take tourists around in safe conditions; this website should also include information on photography and should have all information that a visitor information centre should have.

In the bid to increase tourism in Lagos, Okupe's team was also mindful of avoiding an increase in traffic, and to encourage environmental sustainability for the residents in Lagos. Okupe wanted the team to keep in mind that the residents were also an essential consideration when making tourism plans and decisions. The tourism plan needed to be ambitious to reflect what Okupe's team could do to provide a renewed sense of living and connection with people in Lagos.

Additional barriers for the project the consulting team anticipated included some tourism stakeholders' lack of understanding and awareness of the tourism system, which led them to think about their own businesses or priorities rather than the potential for partnership and collaboration. This lack of understanding was expected to be a potential issue in the future.

Okupe looked at the first draft six-week plan and considered how to develop it further so the team would have a clear plan of action ahead. Furthermore, they needed to advance the work on a rebrand for Lagos as part of the project and agreed that this aspect of the tourism plan was an integral foundation for all that would be actioned moving forward. How should they proceed, and what could they focus on as they planned for their six-week consulting work?

## Discussion Questions

1. Who is currently motivated (push factors) to travel to Nigeria and Lagos?
2. What is currently de-motivating international travel to Lagos?
3. What destination attributes (pull factors) are identified in the case?
4. Review Week 2 and Week 3 from the six-week plan in Exhibit 6.1; how would you achieve the goal for those weeks?
5. In what ways could the development of tourism in Lagos contribute to economic sustainability?
6. Considering a rebrand of Lagos, what is at the heart of Lagos as a destination (people, experiences, natural environment, etc.) and how might that be translated into the rebrand?

**Learning Activity: Familiarisation Tour of Lagos**

A useful learning activity or preparatory activity for this case is an online familiarisation tour of Lagos.

Consider the destination attributes for Lagos in the case. With these attributes in mind, watch the YouTube video; *Lagos: Vibrant City in Nigeria Must-sees in One of Africa's Most Exciting Cities.* Make notes from the video that expand or deepen your understanding of the destination attributes in Lagos.

Suggested Video for this activity:

Aina T. (n.d). *Lagos: Vibrant City in Nigeria | Must-sees in One of Africa's Most Exciting Cities with @TayoAinaFilms* [Video]. https://www.youtube.com/watch?v=VJnu7lR4Kks

## Notes

1 Bankole, A. S. (2002). The Nigerian tourism sector: Contribution, constraints, and opportunities. *The Journal of Hospitality Financial Management, 10*(1), 71–89.
2 Uzuegbu, J. O. (2012). Tourism as a tool for re-branding Nigeria. *International Journal of Research in Arts and Social Sciences, 4*, 404–414.
3 Uzuegbu, J. O. (2012). Tourism as a tool for re-branding Nigeria. *International Journal of Research in Arts and Social Sciences, 4*, 404–414.
4 BOP Consulting. (n.d.). *Number of international tourists per year.* World City Culture Forum. Available at: http://www.worldcitiesculturefor um.com/data/number-of-international-tourists-per-year
5 Tourism Economics. (2021). *Driving and the tourism recovery in Nigeria: Data and digital platforms.* Amazon AWS. Available at: https://s3.amazonaws.com/tourism-economics/craft/Google_Nigeria_Final.pdf

## References and Further Reading


Aina T. (n.d). *Lagos: Vibrant city in Nigeria | Must-sees in one of Africa's most exciting cities with @TayoAinaFilms* [Video]. Available at: https://www.youtube.com/watch?v=VJnu7lR4Kks

Bankole, A. S. (2002). The Nigerian tourism sector: Contribution, constraints, and opportunities. *The Journal of Hospitality Financial Management, 10*(1), 71–89.

BOP Consulting. (n.d.). *Number of international tourists per year.* World City Culture Forum. Available at: http://www.worldcitiesculturefor um.com/data/number-ofinternational-tourists-per-year

Dean, D., & Suhartanto, D. (2019). The formation of visitor behavioral intention to creative tourism: The role of push–pull motivation. *Asia Pacific Journal of Tourism Research, 24*(5), 393–403. Available at: https://doi.org/10.1080/10941665.2019.1572631

Obieluem, U. H., & Okpoko, P. U. (2017). Impacts of religious tourism in southeastern Nigeria. *Journal of Tourism and Heritage Studies, 6*(1), 99–112.

Ogunberu, F. A. (2011). *Socio-economic impact of tourism development in Nigeria case study of tourist attractions along the coastline of Lagos* [Thesis]. Central Ostrobothnia University of Applied Sciences.

Tourism Economics. (2021). *Driving and the tourism recovery in Nigeria: Data and digital platforms.* Amazon AWS. Available at: https://s3.amazonaws.com/tourismeconomics/craft/Google_Nigeria_Final.pdf

Uysal, M., Li, X., & Sirakaya-Turk, E. (2008). Push-pull dynamics in travel decisions. In H., Oh (Ed.), *Handbook of hospitality marketing management*, (pp. 412–439). Routledge.

Uzuegbu, J. O. (2012). Tourism as a tool for re-branding Nigeria. *International Journal of Research in Arts and Social Sciences, 4*, 404–414.

## Exhibits

**Exhibit 6.1** First Draft Red Clay Advisory Work Plan

| Schedule | Work Plan |
|---|---|
| Week 1 | Understand what was happening with the Commissioner for Lagos State Ministry of Culture and the Ministry's expectations; also speak with different stakeholders. |
| Week 2 | Distill the tourism plan objectives and get feedback on them from key stakeholders. |
| Week 3 | Arrive at the distilled focus for the themes and goals for the masterplan. |
| Week 4 | Develop a stakeholder engagement and management plan. |
| Week 5 | Communicate with investors and other financiers for investments in the LSTMP and future branding projects. |
| Week 6 | Attend workshops with the stakeholders to discuss the plan and explore assumptions and perspectives. Provide time and opportunity for stakeholders to comment and give feedback. |

Source: Red clay advisory with permission.

**Exhibit 6.2** International Tourism, Number of Arrivals – Nigeria

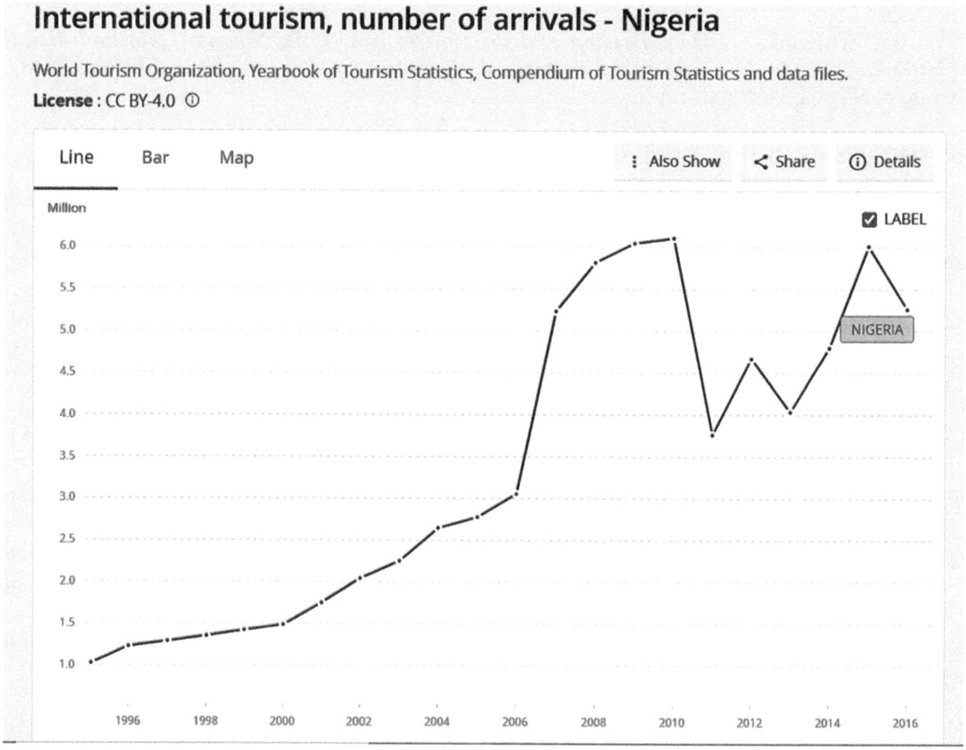


Source: World tourism organization, yearbook of tourism statistics, compendium of tourism statistics and data files. License: CCBY-4.0.

**Exhibit 6.3** Domestic vs International Stays in Nigeria

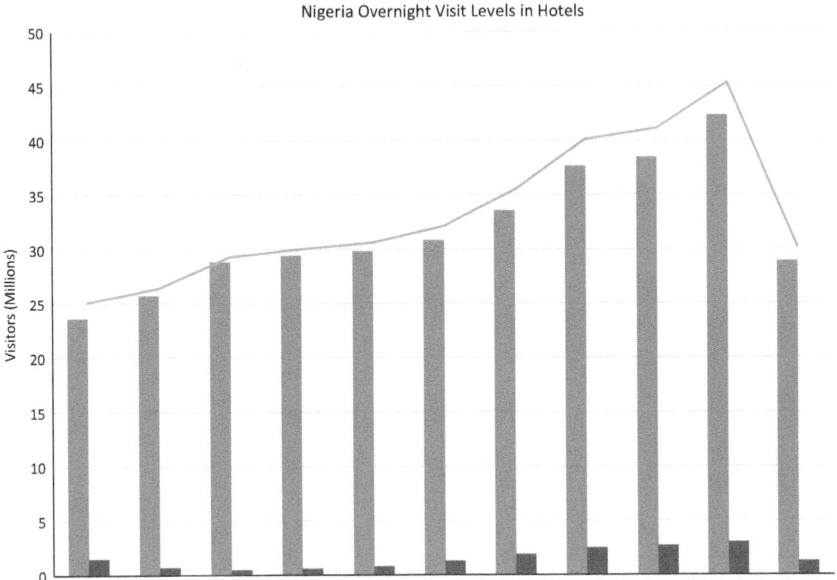


| | 2010 | 2011 | 2012 | 2013 | 2014 | 2015 | 2016 | 2017 | 2018 | 2019 | 2020 |
|---|---|---|---|---|---|---|---|---|---|---|---|
| Domestic | 23.6 | 25.7 | 28.8 | 29.4 | 29.8 | 30.8 | 33.5 | 37.6 | 38.4 | 42.3 | 28.9 |
| International | 1.5 | 0.7 | 0.5 | 0.6 | 0.8 | 1.3 | 1.9 | 2.5 | 2.7 | 3 | 1.3 |
| Total Overnight visits | 25.1 | 26.4 | 29.3 | 30 | 30.6 | 32.1 | 35.4 | 40.1 | 41.1 | 45.3 | 30.2 |

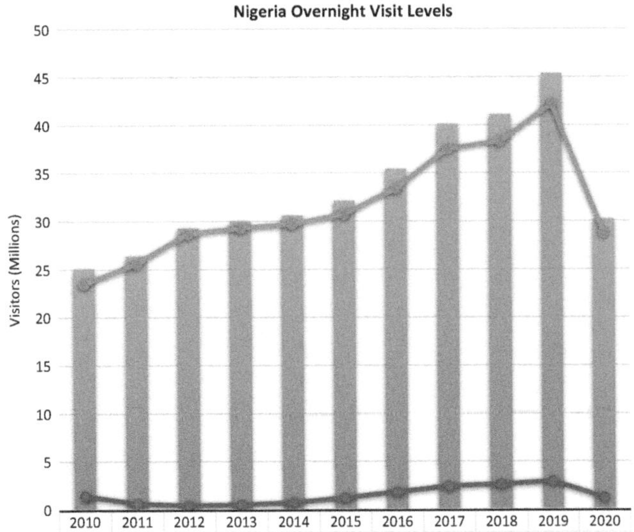


| | 2010 | 2011 | 2012 | 2013 | 2014 | 2015 | 2016 | 2017 | 2018 | 2019 | 2020 |
|---|---|---|---|---|---|---|---|---|---|---|---|
| Total Overnight visits | 25.1 | 26.4 | 29.3 | 30 | 30.6 | 32.1 | 35.4 | 40.1 | 41.1 | 45.3 | 30.2 |
| Domestic | 23.6 | 25.7 | 28.8 | 29.4 | 29.8 | 30.8 | 33.5 | 37.6 | 38.4 | 42.3 | 28.9 |
| International | 1.5 | 0.7 | 0.5 | 0.6 | 0.8 | 1.3 | 1.9 | 2.5 | 2.7 | 3 | 1.3 |

Source: Graph reproduced. Tourism economics and UNWTO.

**Exhibit 6.4** Map of Lagos

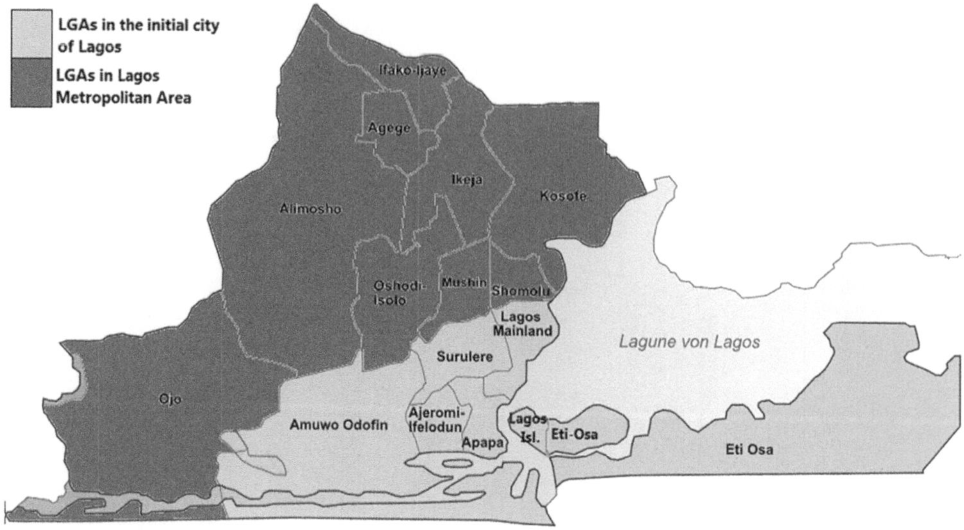


Source: Commons Wikimedia.

Bohr (https://commons.wikimedia.org/wiki/File:Map_of_the_Local_Government_Areas_of_Lagos.png), "Map of the Local Government Areas of Lagos", https://creativecommons.org/licenses/by-sa/3.0/legalcode

# CASE 7

## LOCAL I'A

### A Social Enterprise Makes a Big Impact on a Small Scale

*Jonelle Knowles*

**Synopsis**

This case study examines Local I'a, a social enterprise that operated as a sustainable fresh seafood retailer. Local I'a sourced seafood and products from local fishers, with a model of purchasing seasonal local seafood at a fair market value directly from the fishers and selling direct to restaurant and individual consumers. At the heart of sustainable "pono" fishing practices is emphasising the importance of respecting the environment and maintaining a balance between human activities and nature. While the concept was admired by sustainable food advocates and the media, Ashley Watts, owner of Local I'a believed more impact could be made, especially with the restaurant industry sector.

In November of 2021, Local I'a had operated for many years as a sustainable fresh seafood retailer on the island of Oahu in the Hawaiian island state. The meaning of I'a was "fish" in the native Hawaiian language. Local I'a sourced its seafood from local fishers who held shared values. Local I'a approached sustainability with a unique "dock to dish" model and purchased, at a fair market value, seasonal local seafood directly from the fishers and sold direct to the consumer, both individual customers and restaurants. While the concept was admired by sustainable food advocates and the media, Ashley Watts, owner of Local I'a believed more impact could be made.

Sustainable fishing in the Hawaiian Islands was essential to the preservation of the marine ecosystem and to the livelihood of the local communities. Fishing was deeply ingrained in Hawaiian culture and had been an integral part of their way of life for centuries. Unsustainable fishing practises, overfishing, and climate change had impacted fish stocks and threatened the sustainability of the industry. In response, the Hawaiian government in their Hawai'i Ocean Management Plan (2020) identified a goal to *"promote fishing practices that adopt the wisdom of both traditional ecological knowledge and scientific ecological knowledge to*

DOI: 10.4324/9781003280040-11

*improve fish stocks.*" To promote sustainable fishing practices and ensure the long-term viability of the fishery industry, creative solutions and approaches were needed.

Local I'a took a quadruple-bottom line approach, seeking to create positive environmental, social, economic, and cultural changes in the island community. The overarching goal was to support sustainable fishing livelihoods by increasing the value of local fisheries; to improve consumer access to fresh, local, responsibly caught seafood; and to preferentially source from sustainable fisheries that were well-managed and could provide seafood for future generations.

Growth of the Local I'a operation was limited by the number of skilled employees, inadequate physical space and cold storage, the distribution strategy for the restaurant industry, and brand identity and marketing. There were opportunities to expand the local customer base and build a network within the restaurant sector, to help build greater awareness for Local I'a and the sustainability principles the operation followed.

## Pono Fishing Practices

The traditional Hawaiian concept of "mālama 'āina," to care for the land, was at the heart of sustainable fishing practices, and emphasised the importance of respecting the environment and maintaining a balance between human activities and nature. "Pono," a Hawaiian word that expressed the values that motivated one to strive for this balance, described this type of practice that inherently placed sustainability at the forefront. Pono was an important cultural concept that had several English definitions, but none of them fully capture its meaning. Most definitions, conveyed the idea of righteousness and balance.

## Local I'a, Core Elements of Pono Fishing Standards

The values of pono on the Local I'a website were stated as:

- All seafood is sourced from healthy stocks, and fishers fish in ways that allow populations to replenish themselves.
- Fishers take care of the resource and minimise the impact of their fishing activities on the environment.
- Fishers adhere to state and federal fishing regulations and are active participants in improving management systems

## Ashley Watts

Ashley Watts settled in Hawaii in 2007 on the island of Oahu. Watts held a bachelor of science in marine biology from the University of West Florida and a master's in zoology from Miami University. Watts hailed from a fishing family in Florida. Her focus as a master's student was community engagement and marine conservation and ecology. As a project while at Miami University, she created an informal educational program on marine ecology, conservation, and how we all can make a difference.

When she first arrived in Hawaii, Watts spent seven years on the ocean working with the Pacific Islands Region Observer program as a fisheries observer on the commercial long line vessels out of Honolulu. She also held a role as a liaison with the fishers. This inspired her passion for the local fishing industry and a commitment to see change in the sustainable practices in the seafood business. She began to work for Local I'a in 2015 and later became owner and managing partner. She operated the ambitious Oahu business almost single-handedly.

## Sustainability and the Local I'a Mission

The mission for Local I'a shared by Watts was "*To increase accessibility and consumption of locally sourced seafood while improving profitability for producers and sustainability in our local fisheries.*" The mandate of this operation focused on all four pillars of sustainability, which included social equity and cultural vitality, as well as economic viability and environmental responsibility.

The Sustainable Development Goals (SDGs), developed by the United Nations, were a call to action to end poverty and inequality, protect the planet, and ensure that all people enjoyed health, justice, and prosperity. Local I'a contributed to several of these SDG's (Exhibit 7.1) by promoting sustainable fishing practices to protect marine ecosystems, conserve fish stocks, and prevent overfishing. Fishing was only for species in season and utilised selective fishing methods that reduced bycatch and minimised the impact on the environment. Through awareness campaigns Local I'a educated visitors and locals and encouraged sustainable purchase choices.

## Local I'a Operations

The business operated with a skeleton staff and adopted a complete vertical integration from the time of acquiring the catch. Everything from the purchasing, receiving, cold storage, fish processing, portioning, packaging, selling, and delivering was part of the Local I'a service. Watts herself managed the business and daily operations. She determined business strategies and conceptualised and established the supply chain model. The narrow scope of marketing activities was also in her domain. Her regular tasks included connecting and maintaining relationships with fishers; accepting, weighing, and writing purchasing receipts for their catch; and promoting, selling, and sometimes delivering orders. For this, Watts as owner, didn't draw a personal salary from the company. Embedded in this value chain was the fish processing and packaging that was assisted by one part time employee. With over 16 years of experience as a fish cutter for a major processing and distribution company, his proficiency allowed him to accomplish in a couple of days per week what it might take a novice all week to perform.

To help keep costs low, Watts relied on support from willing people in the industry who believed in the concept and made time to participate. For example, a chef assisted by creating recipes for value added customer communications and created additional product lines, like the Local I'a Seafood Gumbo. Pet treats made from the left-over fish helped to use the whole product more efficiently, while creating an alternate revenue source.

All of this took place out of a small but efficient kitchen space and parking lot in the back of the Kaimuki Superette. To minimise cost and maximise capacity, this space was shared with several small businesses on a rotating schedule. If you were on site for the day, you might smell vegan donuts baking in the early morning or see noodles being made, before the "master fish processor" arrived to descale, cut, and package the seafood.

Local I'a accepted fresh caught fish seven days per week at the business location, and occasionally Watts would pick up as well (Exhibit 7.6). Fishers were paid a consistent and fair price for their catch, often more than they would have received from the wholesale buyers. After processing, fish were sold in several ways. Some fish were sold to a limited number of local restaurants. Fresh fish, frozen fish and prepared foods could be purchased directly from the Local I'a shop during limited operational hours, one day per week. Most fish were sold to individual consumers through a Consumer Supported Fishery (CSF) subscription program with convenient pick up at local farmers' markets. Watts estimated about 25% of their volume was sold to restaurant clients and 75% to community members.

## The Consumer Supported Fishery

The consumer supported fishery (CSF) was a concept that had been used in places around the world and relied on local consumers committed to consuming and supporting local seafood. Some CSF operators pre-sold shares to a fisher's catch, while others like Local I'a, had consumers commit and pre-pay for a regular subscription. The seafood in the subscription boxes supplied, would change with sustainable seasonal availability and the catch of the week. For distribution, Local I'a made use of various locations, including several Farmers' Markets located in different neighbourhoods around the island (Exhibit 7.2), to distribute the subscription boxes. This involved supportive partnerships with other vendors. Most products sales were sold through these subscription packages directly to consumers.

## Restaurants Industry Purchasing

Restaurant delivery took place seven days per week, with a limited number of restaurants on the island that regularly used the service. A restaurant called Fete that lived their sustainable values, included a Local I'a "catch of the day" on their menu. One of the challenges many restaurants faced was that Local I'a could not provide a year-round consistent supply of a specific type of fish for their regular menu. Sustainable fishery included seasonal changes to catch and sustainable access to certain species of fish was limited at certain times. Acceptance of these ideas involved promoting the benefits and responsibilities to restaurateurs and the public, as well as educating tourists and diners to understand why their favourite seafood may not be consistently available.

Consistently keeping up with the high-volume demand from restaurants such as the Four Seasons Resort at Ko Olina or the Ritz Carlton Residences at Waikiki Beach prevented further expansion into the restaurant market (Exhibits 7.3, 7.4, and 7.5). Even if they had access to the amount of product necessary, budgeting for increased resources and staff needed to process that volume would remain a challenge.

One of the advantages for a restaurant that used seafood from Local I'a was a trackable system whereby the restaurant could promote and share online information with the tag line, "know the story of your seafood." Fish sold to restaurants were also given a QR code that provided the restaurant with information on the species of fish, why it would be considered sustainable, and a story about the local fisher responsible for the catch. This could then be shared with restaurant staff to build their personal knowledge and assist them in enlightening and educating their guests. Alternatively, it could be placed in the menu to help to encourage tourists and diners to make responsible choices and add value to their experience while promoting hyper-local ingredients.

The cost and time necessary for Local I'a to maintain this value-added feature was difficult to sustain without an increase in restaurant sales, and an economy of scale, to justify it. While the concept was admirable and well lauded by advocates and the media, Watt's believed that greater impact was possible. Obstacles imposed by limitations in financial and human resources restricted the scope of the operation. The decision whether to scale up the operation to reach a wider audience would have an impact on the location, the human resource needs, the financial investment, and even the amount of seafood being extracted from the local waters. Should Local I'a expand or fine-tune their operations, and if so, what was the best way forward?

### Discussion Questions

1 What makes Local I'a a social enterprise?
2 What are the pros and cons of making this business model at Local I'a scalable?
3 What are the needs of various stakeholders?
4 How are the four pillars of sustainability reflected in the social enterprise at Local I'a?
5 Explain the practises at Local I'a that relate to the UN sustainable development goals. How could these be enhanced for greater impact?

### Learning Activity: Explain How Pono is Reflected in the Case

Read the detailed description from the Local I'a website on "Pono Fishing Standards" that highlights the specifics of Pono as applied to the fisher partners.

Watch the 25-minute "Fishing Pono" video. This video tells the story of a community's struggle to save a diminishing resource, their fishing grounds, on the island of Moloka'i. The video highlights the importance of acknowledging Indigenous knowledge in the struggle to maintain balance and assist in the recovery of fishing habitats.

### Thought Questions

1 In what ways does Local I'a reflect Pono values?
2 What are the potential challenges that might occur in integrating Pono values at Local I'a?

## Video Resources

Local I'a Fish Story https://youtu.be/LYhH32tUTk4 The story of Local I'a
Local I'a Part 2 https://youtu.be/j95BABWy6VY The story of Watts Watts
Fishing Pono (2013) https://vimeo.com/kuahawaii/fishingpono2013 Award-winning film, tells the story of a community's struggle to save a diminishing resource, their fishing grounds, on the island of Moloka'i.

## Acknowledgement

The author wishes to thank Ashley Watts, owner and managing partner of Local I'a, for sharing information, her time, and perspective in November 2021 and May 2023.

## References and Recommended Readings

Lawai'a Pono: Community-Based Fishing by Ted Kawahinehelelani Blake & Charles Young

*Lawai'a pono—to fish in a Hawaiian way—isn't about the take. Rather, it's about taking care. Lawai'a pono is about our responsibility to practice restraint and make sacrifices today for the long-term benefit of generations to follow.* Available at: https://kamehamehapublishing.org/wp-content/uploads/sites/38/2020/09/Hulili_Vol11_5.pdf

Pono fishing standards (Local I'a). Available at: http://localiahawaii.com/resources/pono-fishing-standards

*A detailed description of Local I'a fishing standards that incorporate indigenous Hawaiian fishing practises and social principles for ethically sourced food with the integration of globally recognised industry standards for environmentally sustainable seafood.*

Rostron, K. I. (2015). Defining the social enterprise: A tangled web. *International Journal of Management and Applied Research*, *2*(2), 85–99. Avaialble at: https://doi.org/10.18646/2056.22.15-007

## Exhibits

### **Exhibit 7.1** United Nations Relevant Sustainable Development Goals (SDG's)

SDG 14: Life Below Water: This goal aims to conserve and sustainably use the oceans, seas, and marine resources. (UN.org) Sustainable fishing practices in the Hawaiian Islands align with this goal by promoting sustainable fishing practices that protect marine ecosystems, conserve fish stocks, and prevent overfishing.

SDG 12: Responsible Consumption and Production: This goal aims to promote sustainable consumption and production patterns (UN.org). Sustainable fishing practices in the Hawaiian Islands aligned with this goal by fishing only for species in season and promoting the use of selective fishing methods that reduced bycatch and minimized the impact on the environment. Some of these methods included traditional fishing practises that helped promote cultural preservation and the passing down of knowledge. Making sustainable seafood available to the public contributed to their ability to make sustainable consumer choices and further the understanding of what that could look like.

SDG 8: Sustainable Tourism: The World Tourism Organization defines sustainable tourism as "tourism that takes full account of its current and future economic, social, and environmental impacts, addressing the needs of visitors, the industry, the environment and host communities." This is related to the education of visitors about sustainable fishery and on making responsible consumption choices.

Source: United Nations SDGs.

### **Exhibit 7.2** Retail Sales & Seafood Community Supported Fishery (CSF) Subscription Pickup Locations

Local I'a Kitchen in Kaimuki
3458 Waialae Ave
Honolulu, HI 96816
Retail Sales Saturday 10–3 pm & CSF Pickup Friday & Saturday

Kokua Market Coop
2643 S King St
Honolulu, HI 96812
CSF pickup Friday 12–6 pm

HFBF Farmers' Market at Mililani High School
95-1200 Meheula Pkwy
Mililani HI 96789
CSF pickup and Retail Sales Sundays 8–11am

Hawaii Kai on the Fly
Moanalua Boatramp (currently at our fishmonger's house)
CSF Pickup Friday 12:30-dark

Kailua, HI 96734
CSF pickup at a CSF members' house Friday 2–7 pm in Enchanted Lakes

Farmlink
Get our fish, local produce and other items delivered to your door! (EBT accepted)
CSF pickup & retail sales

Kalapawai Kailua Beach
306 S Kalaheo Ave
Kailua 96734
CSF Pickup *COMING SOON*

**Exhibit 7.3** Restaurant Clients

Mud Hen Water
3452 Waialae Ave, Honolulu, HI 96816
Fete Restaurant Honolulu
2 North Hotel St, Honolulu Hi 96817
Koko Head Café
1120 12th Ave, Honolulu, Hi 96816
Mina's Fish House (Four Season's Resort)
La Vie (Ritz Carlton)

Source: Ashley Watts.

**Exhibit 7.4** Local I'a Store Front

(a) (b)

Source: Author's photograph.

**Exhibit 7.5** Fish in Crate

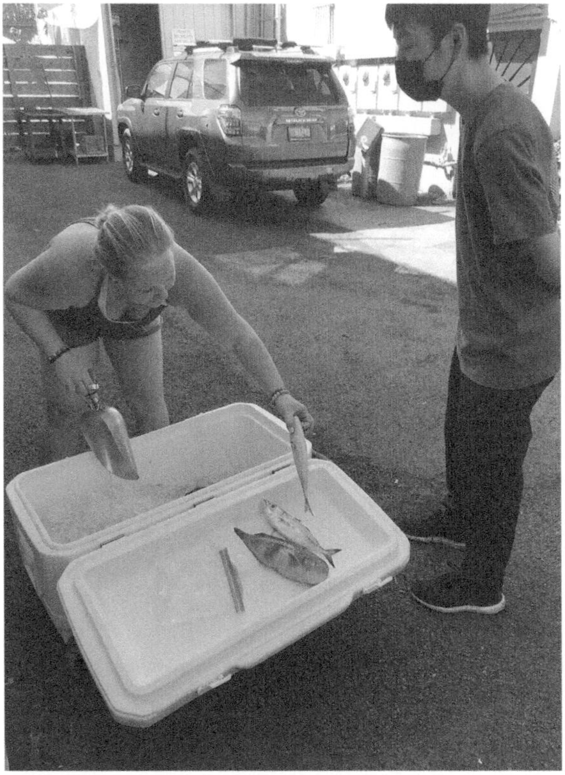

Source: Author's photograph.

# PART 3

# Operations Management

Bringing international cases from Australia, Austria, Canada, the USA and Vietnam, these cases profile a range of operational issues faced by small business owners.

DOI: 10.4324/9781003280040-12

# CASE 8

## THE PEAK HOTEL

### The Challenge of Succession and Family Firm Continuity

*Anita Zehrer, Gabriela Leiß, Charles Krusekopf, and Rebecca Wilson-Mah*

**Synopsis**

A family-run four-star hotel in the Austrian Alps had challenges with family firm succession. The family firm was in its second generation, and the owners, Perry and Patricia, wanted to develop a plan to hand the business to the next generation. The entrepreneurial family was dealing with change and transformation processes among the family members.

On the eve of their 38th wedding anniversary in June 2017, as Perry and Patricia sat down on their sunny patio for their regular afternoon coffee, each could see the worry in the other's eyes. They were the successful owners of a family-run hotel, the Peak Hotel, in Lermoos, a bustling Austrian ski town, but knew they had to make some major decisions. On considering the 38-year milestone she was celebrating with Perry, Patricia said:

> Perry, I am not sure how many years we have left together. We have two sons; let's turn the business over to them and spend our remaining years doing things together rather than always working.

Perry understood and sympathised with his wife's ideas but was not sure how to achieve her wishes. The couple inherited the hotel from Patricia's parents when it was a small farm inn, and through hard work and keen market insight they had transformed the property over the past 35 years into a large four-star hotel that had become well known among European families seeking a holiday offering rest, relaxation, and wellness. Perry still loved working, and he was unsure that his sons had the skills and dedication to maintain the business at the same level that he and his wife had achieved. His sons and their spouses were very different people, and it was often difficult to get the family members to agree. He could not understand how they would jointly manage a complex operation such as the hotel.

DOI: 10.4324/9781003280040-13

Reflecting on these relationships Perry said:

> Patricia, I feel that your family gave us a great inheritance, and through our hard work we have earned the right to retire and spend more time together. However, if we want to retire we must create a plan that ensures the success of this hotel so that we can fund our retirement and honour the inheritance that your family gave to us and that we built into what it is today.

## The Peak Hotel

The Peak Hotel was founded as a farm inn by Patricia's parents in 1965 when Lermoos was a small village in the Austrian Alps. In 1982, when it had 16 staff people and 50 small rooms, the inn was passed down to Patricia and her young husband Perry. The inn offered a basic bed and breakfast, and, initially, the couple maintained the style of the inn. Later, in the 1980s, with the trend toward a focus on the special interests of guests, the couple began to focus more on families and decided to enhance the hotel by adding rooms and services. Over the next 30 years they transformed the small inn into a high-end four-star family resort that catered to wealthy European families on holiday. Patricia and Perry were leading hospitality innovators in Lermoos and helped develop the small village into a well-known four-season resort destination. In the 1990s, the Peak had been one of the first Lermoos hotels that began focusing on families and the development of a whole-family wellness offering. This required substantial investment and was seen as a new and risky undertaking, but their entrepreneurial risk-taking paid off, and the hotel progressively added rooms and services and expanded its market. The most recent upgrade occurred in 2016 when the hotel invested €13 million in a new outdoor wellness area, room refurbishments, and a high-end restaurant.

In 2017 the hotel hosted 114,000 overnight stays, an increase of over 8% from the year before. It primarily drew from a regional market with 75% of customers from neighbouring Switzerland and Germany, and 10% from Benelux countries. The remainder came from Austria and other European states. Annual revenue in 2017 was €14 million, with earnings before taxes of €3.2 million. In 2017, the net profit ratio was 20.8%, the return on assets were 12.3%. The equity ratio was 50.85% in 2016/2017 compared to 39.82% in 2015/2016 with a return on equity of 25.6% in 2016/2017 compared to 24.5% in 2015/2016. In 2017, the indirect debt-repayment period was calculated with 3.1 years for the economic year 2016/2017 compared to 4.9 years in 2015/2016. The hotel employed 90 staff full time, and over 130 in peak times, including 5 managers. Staff costs were 26.8% of their overall expenses with an operating efficiency of €175,000 and staff costs per employee of €47,000. It had strong staff loyalty and retention with an annual employee turnover rate of 20%, which was far below the average within the Lermoos tourism sector.

A year-round destination, Lermoos was in the Tirolean Alps in Austria with a population of approximately 1,000 permanent residents. The destination was among the most renowned family destinations in Europe, both summer and winter alike. The Peak Hotel was one of the most renowned accommodation providers in the destination, and Perry and Patricia had been leaders within the Lermoos destination management organisation helping to build a brand that identified Lermoos as a family friendly location that offered high-quality accommodations, excellent service, and a diverse set of mountain holiday activities. The Peak Hotel was one of the first hotels in the region to offer enhanced wellness and spa services, and the 2016 expansion of these services kept the Peak Hotel at the forefront of high-end accommodations within the destination.

### About Patricia and Perry and Their Family

Patricia, age 57, and Perry, age 61, were the owners of the Peak Hotel. A few years after meeting and getting married, when they both were studying in hotel school, Patricia inherited the hotel from her parents, and the young couple began to make changes to expand the hotel into a larger and more professionally run operation. After handing over the hotel, Patricia's parents withdrew from any involvement in the hotel, as they sometimes clashed with Perry about his new ideas, and they moved on to work with another business. Patricia and Perry invested into the hotel infrastructure as well as in accommodations for their employees. Over time, Patricia and Perry's vision of a larger, high-end family resort hotel took hold and proved to be successful, and the couple and hotel became well-respected members of the local tourism establishment. In 2009, they became a member of the Leading Family Hotels and Resorts, a group of luxury family resorts in Austria and Italy, and invested in enhanced services such as extended opening hours or night reception.

At the hotel, Perry served as hotel director overseeing all operations, while Patricia managed reservations and bookings. Patricia and Perry had two sons, Charles and Peter, who were now both in their late 20s and early 30s and married. While the kids were growing, Patricia always had the dream that their two sons would take over the business, although she had wanted to make sure that family harmony was not compromised the way it was between her husband and her parents. She was also concerned about the extensive social responsibility taken by their family towards their employees and the larger community. Reflecting on what she valued about the family business Patricia said:

> The history and the tradition of our family business are very important to me. Thus, I fear that conflicts among Perry, Charles, and Peter might tear the business apart, which would also endanger the reputation of the hotel and the family.

Perry felt unsure about letting go of his role as head of the hotel. He had always exerted a very patriarchal leadership style, and still found himself to be full of energy and entrepreneurial spirit. While discussing retirement with Patricia, Perry exclaimed:

> While part of me welcomes the change, the transition, the other part says I will miss it like hell!

The most crucial question for him was the commitment of his sons to the business. He was concerned that his sons would not find their way in the family business and might not be 100% committed to a lifetime at the Peak Hotel. His elder son, Charles, and his wife, Susan, both worked as managers in the business. However, Perry observed that when the last guest left, at the end of the season, Charles and Susan took their holidays and did not stay around to oversee the property and prepare it for winter (Exhibit 8.1).

His younger son, Peter, and his wife, Olivia, had no real experience working in a hotel, although they recently expressed an interest in returning to Lermoos to help run the family business (Exhibit 8.1). He and Patricia had always been 100% committed to the hotel. They were willing to do any job that was necessary to keep the hotel running and would have never left for holidays until the hotel had been closed up and everything wrapped up.

Perry was torn between his wife's desires to retire, and his own feelings that he needed to keep running the business for at least a few more years until his sons were ready to take over. He was determined to maintain the integrity and strength of the family business and the brand that he and his wife had developed. As a small business owner, he also knew that the hotel was his retirement plan; therefore, it was important to him that the hotel remained financially successful so that he and Patricia could get maximum value out of the hotel to support their retirement. Perry and Patricia have saved money, but this capital is bound in a foundation, which they set up years ago with 76% of ownership on Perry and 24% of ownership on Patricia; thus, the success of the family business determines the amount of their pension when they go into retirement. This means, Perry and Patricia will receive earnings from the successors based on the successfulness of the business. Perry's perspective was summarised in the statement he made about his mission:

> My mission is to make the right decisions and reduce the misunderstandings among the family members so we can start the succession process and put the hotel on a path to continued success.

## The Next Generation

For the past five years, Perry and Patricia's elder son, Charles, had been a division manager overseeing operations at the Peak Hotel, and his wife, Susan, was the manager of the reception desk. Both of them had been educated in a highly renowned hotel school in Switzerland, and they were deeply integrated into the local Lermoos community together with their two young daughters, aged 1 and 3 (Exhibit 8.1). Charles was a member of the volunteer fire brigade and joined several village clubs and associations. During Charles and Susan's wedding, which was held in Lermoos, Patricia and Peter had announced their intention to pass the hotel along to Charles and Susan. After their wedding, Charles and Susan had always planned their lives around the idea that one day they would take over the Peak Hotel. As Charles explained:

> As a young child, I grew up around the business and always looked up to what my parents did. I found it great that they were true hosts and were loved by the guests. This is why I went to a hotel school, to learn how to manage a hotel the right way.

Charles, however, often clashed with his father, who had a very different management style and personality. Charles struggled with the way his father treated him in the business and felt that his father did not trust his competencies. He and his father had very different leadership styles. While Charles liked to delegate decision making and develop strong employee teams, Perry was a very top-down and fact-oriented manager who believed in hierarchical structures. Charles and Susan were also concerned that the business lacked clear policies for employees and needed to develop workplace and job descriptions now that it had over 100 employees. Perry and Charles' relationship had grown so strained that they avoided talking directly to each other and mostly communicated by email. Susan was concerned about how Perry treated Charles, and despite the pledge made at their wedding and their many years working in the business, the couple wondered if they would be better off moving to work at a different hotel or starting a new hotel of their own.

Charles and Susan's concerns about their place in the business grew when Charles' younger brother, Peter, and his wife Olivia, returned to Lermoos in early 2017 to start working at the Peak Hotel. Patricia and Perry's younger son, Peter, had moved away from Lermoos first to attend boarding school and then universities in the United States, Spain, and Switzerland. After graduating from university, Peter worked in a high-paying job in the finance industry in Geneva. There he met his wife, Olivia, who was trained in marketing and worked in marketing management for a number of large companies in Switzerland. Olivia was from Chile and did not speak German but had been raised like Peter in a family that ran their own business. After a few years together in Switzerland, in 2017 the young couple decided they wanted to start a family and felt it was time to move back to Lermoos to join the family business. As Peter explained:

> My friends keep telling me I have a great opportunity to go home and work in our family business. They ask how could you not do it? What an opportunity!

A major factor for Peter and Olivia was the potential that they saw in the business. Peter felt his experience in finance would be a strategic asset the hotel could leverage, and Olivia was sure that her marketing experience would be useful. They felt their wide range of international experiences and contacts could help the Peak Hotel grow and develop new markets and lines of business. They saw that the tourism business was changing, with people taking shorter but more frequent holiday breaks, demanding new experiences. They felt that the hotel had the opportunity to tap into new clientele from a more diverse set of countries in Asia or South America.

There were, however, several factors that made Peter and Olivia's transition back to Lermoos and the Peak Hotel difficult. First, there were no clear positions for either of them at the hotel. Second, the fact that Olivia did not speak German and had always lived in big cities made it difficult for her to integrate and contribute within the Lermoos community. Finally, after Peter and Olivia's return to Lermoos, Peter and Charles and their spouses struggled to develop a working relationship. The two brothers had very different personalities and life experiences. Charles had envied his younger brother since their childhood and felt that their parents had always favoured Peter and made life easier for him, in part because Peter had diabetes.

After Peter returned, Charles was very nervous about his future role at the hotel, and he and Susan had several arguments and difficult moments with Peter and Olivia due to the tension they all felt. Charles and Susan were concerned that Peter and Olivia were trying to come in and take over the Peak Hotel despite not having a strong knowledge of the industry and region. The relationship between the two brothers had never been close, but after Peter's return relations broke down further and the two brothers generally avoided each other and rarely spoke. Both Charles and Peter, and their spouses, had an interest in owning and working at the Peak Hotel. They were sure that they had the skills and experience necessary to successfully run the hotel and continue to expand the hotel's marketing and services.

Everyone had the same goal for the Peak Hotel, to ensure that it remained a family owned and run business that offered a high-quality experience for guests and a comfortable and harmonious life for all the members of the family. Perry thought a great deal about the experiences he and Patricia had together after inheriting the family business. He found that the couple's conversations often returned to discussing their retirement concerns and the future of the hotel. The history and tradition of the family business were very important to Perry. He feared that conflicts between Charles and Peter might tear the business apart, which would also endanger his retirement and the reputation of the hotel and family.

As Patricia and Perry sipped their coffee on a bright June day, Perry decided to call a meeting with their two sons and their wives to begin the succession planning process.

## Discussion Questions

1 What are the challenges of intra-family succession based on the narrative of the given case? Consider both business-related and family-related issues for both generations.
2 What are the strengths, weaknesses, and interests of each of the family members?
3 Identify the key business function issues that are present in the case.
4 What are the options and key steps to consider in family succession?
5 Are there other options for the business the family might consider?

## Learning Activity: Application of a concept of the family-controlled firm

Tagiuri, R., & Davis, J. (1996). Bivalent attributes of the family firm. *Family Business Review, 9*(2), 199–208.

In this article, Tagiuri and Davis (1996) propose that the family-controlled firm has "unique, inherent attributes, and each of these key attributes is a source of benefits and disadvantages for owning families, nonfamily employees, and family employees" (p. 200). This article outlines a Three Circle Model that identifies graphically three sets of relationships in the family firm: owners, managers and employees, and family members. Within this conceptual model Tagiuri and Davis proposed there are unique bivalent attributes that are derived from the overlap of family, ownership, and management relationships. Furthermore, the authors identified bivalent attributes as follows: 1) simultaneous roles, 2) shared identity, 3) a lifeline common history, 4) emotional involvement and confusion, 5) mutual awareness and privacy, and 6) the meaning of the family company. These bivalent attributes are each introduced and explained in the article.

## Directions

Work in a team of three and together consider the case and the bivalent attributes as follows: 1) simultaneous roles, 2) shared identity, 3) a lifeline common history, 4) emotional involvement and confusion, 5) mutual awareness and privacy, and 6) the meaning of the family company.

1 Review the description of the bivalent attributes in the article. Review the case and identify how the bivalent attributes and associated qualities are evident in the case.

2 Identify the negative and positive aspects of these bivalent attributes at the Peak Hotel.
3 Propose how the family can best navigate each attribute for a positive outcome.
4 Which bivalent attributes do you consider to be the most significant in this case?
5 What are the general challenges for a family regarding the identification and navigation of the different bivalent attributes in a family firm?
6 How could an understanding of bivalent attitudes contribute to succession planning?

## References and Suggested Reading

F. F. I. Practitioner (2015). *Family business role models: Understanding role complexity.* Available at: https://ffipractitioner.org/family-business-role-models-understandingrole-complexity/

Leiß, G., & Zehrer, A. (2018). Intergenerational communication in family firm succession. *Journal of Family Business Management*, *8*(1), 75–90

Tagiuri, R., & Davis, J. (1996). Bivalent attributes of the family firm. *Family Business Review*, *9*(2), 199–208.

## Exhibit

**Exhibit 8.1** Background on the Family Members

| | |
|---|---|
| Charles (33) | Education in the field of hospitality; graduated from a highly renowned hotel school in Switzerland; deeply integrated into the local Lermoos community; social person; member of the volunteer fire brigade and several village clubs and associations; division manager in the family business since 2012; knows the family business very well; loves to be a host. |
| Susan (30) | Education in the field of hospitality; graduated from a highly renowned hotel school in Switzerland; married to Charles with two kids; responsible for managing the reception desk since 2013; knows the family business very well; loves to be a host. |
| Peter (27) | Education in finance management at universities in the United States, Spain, and Switzerland; work experience in high-paying jobs in the finance industry in Geneva; no experience in the hospitality industry; not integrated into the village community; started to work in the family business in 2017; sees the family business more as a job than heartfelt wish. |
| Olivia (30) | Educated in marketing management; work experiences in marketing for a number of large companies in Switzerland; no experience in the hospitality industry; international experience; originally from Chile; does not speak German and fears living in the small village community compared to the big cities she lived before; started to work in the family business in late 2017. |

# CASE 9

## MARKETING STRATEGY FOR BUSINESS RECOVERY

### Tours of Exploration, a Travel Agency

*Catherine Evans and Sylvia Paradis*

**Synopsis**

Until early 2020, Catherine Evans, founder and owner of Tours of Exploration, had a successful tour business with both international and domestic clients, for departures within Canada and in Asia, Europe, Africa, Central, and South America. To expand her digital and social marketing Evans had hired a digital marketing coordinator. Her objective was to better position the Tours of Exploration brand, increase engagement and grow her client-base. Things changed abruptly in March 2020, when the pandemic threw chaos on Evans' business. Caught in a no revenue financial situation, with expenses and a heavy workload, and uncertainty ahead, Evans was tasked with determining how to adjust her digital marketing strategy to a recovery pandemic marketing plan for Tours of Exploration. With several alternatives to consider, she had to make a strategic choice.

On May 19, 2020, Catherine Evans, founder and owner of the travel agency Tours of Exploration in British Columbia, Canada, reviewed her sales and marketing numbers. She had 0 bookings and 0 new inquiries and leads, a pattern Evans feared might continue for some time. Since Canada's international border closure on March 16, 2020, the COVID-19 travel restrictions had immediately impacted domestic and international travel and had effectively eliminated all of Tours of Exploration's business. Between March 16 and May 19, 2020, every spare moment of Evans' time had been preoccupied with contacting insurance companies and land partners of destinations around the globe, trying to salvage as much of her clients' booking payments, and securing future travel credits. Evans' clients had either cancelled their upcoming Tours of Exploration trips or cashed in their trips for future travel credits.

Before the pandemic Evans' had an average of six different client bookings, and 30 or more leads per week. With non-essential travel on pause, there was no foreseeable revenue

DOI: 10.4324/9781003280040-14

for the business. Despite the uncertainty, Evans was determined to survive, and on May 19, 2020, Evans decided it was time to develop a new marketing strategy for her business.

## Catherine Evans and Tours of Exploration

2020 was Tours of Exploration's 30th year, and prior to the pandemic, Evans had planned to develop a marketing strategy for her website development and her social media, as well as to refresh her company's brand to better attract a younger demographic. Despite the uncertain future travel climate, Evans was determined to continue a refresh, but now had a new challenging context to consider. Working with a fixed budget, Evans believed that a sound marketing strategy would be key for business recovery should pandemic-related restrictions cease, and she knew that her next steps had to be calculated carefully if her company was to survive.

Evans had founded Tours of Exploration in 1990 following a 15-month solo journey in South-East Asia. Inspired by her travels, Evans was struck with the idea of combining her passions in zoology and anthropology with a type of business that would connect travellers to educational adventures involving wildlife, culture, and sustainability. Her first idea was to set up a research centre in her homebase of Toronto and to focus on sending travellers to South-East Asia and South America, where Evans had first-hand travel experience. After running some feasibility studies, Evans determined that a research centre would not be economically practical. Instead, she purchased the shares of a travel agency and created the travel brand Tours of Exploration to assist travellers with visits in Asia, Australia, South America, and wild regions of Canada.

Owning an agency and founding the brand Tours of Exploration proved a fulfilling outlet for Evans' entrepreneurial spirit. She found ownership offered a greater flexibility and control of her travel experiences. With a passion for travel, coupled with her global network of travel partners that spanned various tourism sectors and businesses, Evans believed she had the right experience and connections to run a successful, independent travel agency. These travel partners included tour operators, destination marketing organisations, transit operators, accommodation providers, and wildlife viewing experts. By early 2020, Tours of Exploration had been heavily booked with upcoming tours lined up for both international and domestic clients. These tours had been enthusiastically preparing for departures within Canada and in Asia, Europe, Africa, Central, and South America. Evans' revenue streams had been steady and predictable.

## Values

Throughout the years, Evans was able to refine her company's key values, which gave her brand and product-line direction. These values also helped to differentiate Tours of Exploration from other travel agencies and were:

- To **enrich lives** through nature, culture, and adventure travel.
- To collaborate closely to create **personalised, customisable itineraries** for their travellers.
- To prioritise **sustainability and wildlife conservation** in their tours.
- To prioritise working with communities to economically **support the chosen area's local populations**, while also guaranteeing an **authentic, culturally immersive experience** for travellers.

These values and Evans' travel experiences seemed to resonate most with the 55+ demographic. Most of her clients were retired, highly educated, and mid-to-high income, and they normally travelled with their immediate family, or in small groups.

Over the years, Evans had learned how to respond to a broad range of travel related issues and was adept at resolving them to her clients' satisfaction. She was able to help her clients sort out visa and travel arrangements, make various insurance claims, and prepare appropriately for a range of destinations and activities. She had navigated the 9/11 tragedy in 2001, and the financial crisis in 2008 – two events that had significant negative impacts on international travel. The COVID-19 pandemic was her latest challenge, and one she believed she would ultimately surmount. When not making travel arrangements for her clients, Evans worked as an associate professor at a local university, where she taught a variety of travel management courses. She was able to share her direct business knowledge and experiences with her students. Through her affiliation with the university, she was also able to access current research and insights on the tourism industry from the university's various networks and library resources.

### The Digital Marketing Coordinator – Stephanie Ortiz

In early 2019, before the onset of COVID-19, Evans' marketing focus was to adopt digital and social marketing to better position the Tours of Exploration brand, grow the client-base, and keep the pre-existing client-base engaged. This strategy had involved hiring a Digital Marketing Coordinator to help her to facilitate this vision. With the new direction in mind, Evans had hired Stephanie Ortiz as her Digital Marketing Coordinator. Much like Evans, Ortiz had a spirited, entrepreneurial mind with an undeniable passion for travel. She already had her own virtual consulting business, where she helped entrepreneurs establish their own brand and marketing strategies. A few months into her position, Ortiz also had the opportunity to experience some of Tours of Exploration's travel itineraries first-hand, and Ortiz had participated in familiarisation trips to Ecuador and the Galapagos Islands.

Holding similar workstyles and values, Evans and Ortiz made a strong team. Where Evans was experienced in organising clients' travel arrangements and operational tasks, Ortiz was able to contribute valuable marketing expertise to help grow Evans' client-base and reach, and to provide recommendations on where to allocate budget and resources. The creation of this digital marketing position had successfully grown the brand and provided opportunities for hiring two additional part-time employees.

### Business Recovery – Moving Forward

Evans recognised that she and the marketing team needed to put their minds together to figure out a new marketing strategy positioned for future business recovery. This would be a challenge – how would they continue to market their travel products in a world that had essentially banned travel? With no precedent to build off, the Tours of Exploration team was uncertain on how to proceed, however, they carried industry knowledge, a good understanding of their client-base, and the knowledge of the theoretical marketing concepts covered in Evans' courses to help guide their decisions. Evans had a marketing budget of $70,000 to allocate across various recovery strategies. Her goal for the recovery plan was to return to pre-pandemic booking levels of 30 inquiries and six bookings per week. If she reached her goal within one year after pandemic measures had ceased, she would consider this campaign a success.

Eager to get started, Evans called a meeting with Ortiz and the rest of the Tours of Exploration team on May 19, 2020, to discuss strategies that could prove effective to recover the travel agency's booking numbers. The proposed strategies they came up with were quite different.

Ortiz suggested:

> We shouldn't halt our marketing procedures now! Now is the time we should be putting our budget into forward-facing marketing more than ever. Clients are currently uncomfortable with the idea of travel. We need to sell them the dream – continue to strategically plant ideas and the future promise of destinations, so that when travel opens back up, our clients are ready to respond. Familiarisation trips with smaller influencers could be especially effective right now. People tend to move in flocks. If they see on social media that Catherine, myself, or anyone else is going on one of our tours, they will feel ever-so-slightly more comfortable with the thought of travel. Their exposure to our familiarisation trips will increase their knowledge of familiar and new destinations, and when the time comes, they will be equipped with the understanding of travel conditions, rules, and regulations, and be comfortable to book with us. Familiarisation trips are a good way to spend our budget.

Aiden Carter, one of the two new part-time marketing employees added:

> Well, to build off that point, we would need an adept social media marketing strategy. Social media is one of the most powerful ways to convey company messaging, including that of influencers! It is also inexpensive – for organic social media, we essentially only need to pay for the labour costs of managing it. However, paid social media is another story – but it's worthwhile to consider as well. Paid advertising would be very effective in building our channels.

Evans saw the issue in a different light and said:

> While I see your points, I'm hesitant about how that will go over with our existing client-base who have been used to receiving promotional material through direct mail brochures, or email newsletters. We need to walk on eggshells here, especially since we don't know how long this pandemic is going to go on for. I think we should plan to put a chunk of our budget into rebranding which could include redesigning our logo, brand, messaging, and web design. We should also focus on organic SEO for our website and do the research to come up with a new strategy to attract a wider demographic. Up until now, our clients have been in the older and retired age range, the majority over the age of 55+. I worry that this is the exact demographic that will fear travel the most, even after the pandemic has settled. Not to mention, they may be of the age where they retire from travel altogether. Why don't we take this time to freshen up our image and come up with a new brand design, logo, and additions to our product-line that would attract a younger, and more localised demographic. We would

> be targeting a slightly younger traveller, 45+ years, predominantly from Canada and the United States. This traveller would continue to prioritise sustainable travel and continue to be drawn to the natural world and active adventure itineraries. This would be reflected this in the new tour packages we will release, alongside our brand launch, which will be predominantly Canadian tours. We need to stay local and advertise domestic tours only at first, as we are uncertain about the future of international travel. Our social media presence will be a direct reflection of these changes, shifting our messaging to reflect our new brand direction. What do you say?

Ortiz wasn't so sure. She wasn't confident that Canadians and Americans of any age would rely on travel agencies to book their close to home trips. While the thought of re-branding excited her, she was unsure that shifting Tours of Exploration's product line to predominantly offer trips in Canada would be a wise next move. She thought, *"Why not continue to promote more of the international trips that worked well in the past?"*

Carter said:

> These are great points, Catherine. Re-branding sure is exciting and I agree that the website needs an overhaul. The first step might be to do a search-engine optimisation (SEO) audit. It would ensure our website is optimised to have engines like Google or Bing pick it up immediately. We want to be amongst the first in the search ranking for new travellers!

The meeting eventually concluded, everyone's mind a-buzz. From the Tours of Exploration team's suggestions, a laundry-list of strategies was consolidated (Exhibit 9.1).

Evans looked at the list of marketing strategies for recovery, and the benefits and costs associated with each one. Given their budget of $70,000, she knew that not all could be implemented, and that some strategies complemented one-another and would work most effectively when used in tandem. She knew she had to make a firm decision, as the unpredictability and stagnancy of the pandemic would cripple her business if she waited for too long. Knowing that her labour and budgeting resources were limited, she believed she could implement some of these solutions, but not all. Now she had the team's input, she made a personal commitment to decide on the strategy choice in the next 48 hours. Her goal for the recovery plan was to move towards securing 30 inquiries and six bookings per week. If she reached her goal within one year after pandemic restrictions had ceased, she would consider her choices for investment a success.

## Discussion Questions

1. In what ways do you notice Evans' values and strengths influencing the business?
2. What are the unique pressures that Evans faced when developing a marketing strategy during the COVID-19 pandemic?
3. Why do you think Tours of Exploration resonated most with a 55+ demographic?
4. Given the range of options Evans' and her team developed for a new marketing strategy (Exhibit 9.1), what would you prioritise and why, and how would you allocate your budget?

### Learning Activity: Onset of the Pandemic

Gössling, S., Scott, D., & Hall, C. M. (2020). Pandemics, tourism and global change: A rapid assessment of COVID-19. *Journal of Sustainable Tourism, 29*(1), 1–20

Read the article written during the onset of the pandemic in April 2020. This article captures the uncertainty of that time frame, which is similar to the timeframe of the case and what was known at the time.

Reflect on the following questions:

1 What crises have affected global tourism in the past, and what is different about the pandemic?
2 When this paper was written in April 2020, list some of the real and expected impacts identified by the authors for key sectors in the tourism industry.
3 Pick one sector identified in the paper, and research the recovery trajectory for that sector.

## References and Suggested Reading

Camilleri, M. A. (2018). "Market segmentation, targeting and positioning." In *Travel marketing, tourism economics and the airline product* (Chapter 4, pp. 69–83). Switzerland: Springer, Cham.

Destination British Columbia (n.d.) *Creating content that drives action along the travel path to purchase*. Available at: https://www.destinationbc.ca/content/uploads/2021/06/DBC-Travel-Path-to-Purchase_FINAL.pdf

Gösling, S., Scott, D., & Hall, C. M. (2020). Pandemics, tourism and global change: A rapid assessment of COVID-19. *Journal of Sustainable Tourism*, *29*(1), 1–20

Morrison, A. M. (2022). *Hospitality and travel marketing*. Taylor & Francis: London

## Exhibit

### Exhibit 9.1 Presented Strategies and Marketing Budget

Budget: Tours of Exploration had a budget of $70,000 to implement towards their recovery marketing strategy.

**Strategy 1: Organize familiarisation (FAM) tours.** This would involve asking an external influencer with a sizable following to attend a Tours of Exploration tour, take video and photography, and make moving social media and blog posts. The goal of a FAM tour would be to amplify Tours of Exploration's products, services, and message to target audiences. Expected outcomes of these tours would be viewers feel more familiar and comfortable booking travel with Tours of Exploration, and asset acquisition (photography, video) that the company can use for some time.

*Cost Quote: If sourcing an external influencer - $10,000 for sourcing the influencer, trip hosting, contract fees, and management of the influencer and the trip. $10,000 per influencer.*

**Strategy 2: Rebrand the company.** This would involve hiring an external design company to refresh and streamline the company's visual identity (logo, brand, typeface) and offer insight into securing a strong, stand-out brand and website. The goal of this would be to make Tours of Exploration more appealing to a younger target audience (45–60) than what they are currently targeting, and to secure Tours of Exploration's competitive advantage in that travel market.

*Cost Quote: Brand design consulting company fees - $10,000.*

**Strategy 3: Update the website and SEO.** NOTE: The website would undergo a search engine optimisation (SEO) audit, with outdated information and new COVID-19 policies being modified along the way. If chosen along with the re-branding (Strategy 2), more time and resources would have to be implemented to keep the brand consistent across all marketing platforms.

Cost *Quote: If no brand-refresh: $10,000 for labour and consulting services.*

*If brand-refresh: $18,000 to cover additional costs of implementing new colours, logo, and branding suggestions.*

**Strategy 4: (Organic) Social Media Marketing.** NOTE: This strategy becomes more expensive the more social platforms Tours of Exploration decides to explore. The goal of social media marketing is to reach new audiences, while amplifying Tours of Exploration's message and current events. While organic social media posts are free; labour costs for a Marketing Manager and asset acquisition, or for example, acquiring rights to photo and video is not. However, it is a great way to support re-branding. Decisions need to be made on which platform is the most worthwhile for Tours of Exploration and their audience.

*Quote: $5,000 per platform. Available platforms: Facebook, Private (community) Facebook Group, Instagram, Twitter, Pinterest, LinkedIn, YouTube, TikTok. Maximum 4 platforms = $ 20,000.*

**Strategy 5: Buy Social Media Advertising.** This involves paying to boost posts for further reach and visibility or paying for ads that appear on social media. As these are inexpensive, a paid social media advertising strategy can be developed. This includes Google ads, Facebook ads, LinkedIn business ads, and others.

*Quote: $300 per ad. Maximum budget allocated over one year: $15,000 (or maximum 50 ads). Double the figure if an advertising agency is hired to implement the paid advertising campaign(s).*

**Strategy 6: New Product Development.** New, mostly domestic tours would be created to better service the new pandemic climate, appealing to a new 35- to 45-year-old target demographic. Thought should be provided on what specific domestic tours should be developed.

*Quote: $3,000 per new product and all associated fees. Maximum new product development budget $15,000 (5 new products).*

**Strategy 7: Market Research.** This involves doing in-house research or contracting an external research company to investigate market trends. This would further the understanding of the playing field Tours of Exploration is working with, including market demands, and a competitor analysis.

*Quote: If in-house research is undertaken, labour cost is $3,750 (150 hours @ $ 25.00 per hour). If an external hire, costs would be $ 6,500 (100 hours @$ 65 per hour).*

**Strategy 8: Contests and Giveaways.** This is most effective when there are social media platforms to work with (Strategy 4). An incentive (a prize) is decided on – usually a Tours of Exploration trip, with a call-to-action for consumers (for example, following a certain channel, subscribing, or spreading the word). This is a great way to promote growth of a social channel and raise awareness. Some thought is needed to decide on the best prize(s) for the contest and giveaway.

*Quote: An effective giveaway campaign would cost $4000. Maximum of three contests or $ 12,000.*

Source: The authors.

# CASE 10

## HERE'S A TIP

### Paying It Forward May Backfire at Oven and Tap

*Sarah Holtzen and Megan Douglas*

**Synopsis**

As part of the leisure and hospitality industry, Oven & Tap, a pizza eatery was included in the food services and drinking places subsector of establishments that prepared food and beverages for immediate consumption (Bureau of Labor Statistics). Workers in this industry were often subjected to specific compensation practises for "tipped" employees. One evening in December Grant Wise, a local real estate marketing entrepreneur dining with 40 business professionals, beamed as he announced, "We are tipping a total of four thousand, four hundred dollars!" This case captures the disagreements and decisions that ensued. The case explores inter-related aspects of compensation, equity theory, tipping policy and procedures, and tip sharing practice in the food and beverage industry in the USA.

It was December 2, 2021, and the festivities of the winter holiday season were in full swing in northwest Arkansas. The dining room was full that evening at the local pizza eatery, Oven & Tap. Grant Wise,[1] a local real estate marketing entrepreneur, dining with 40 business professionals, beamed as he announced, "We are tipping a total of four thousand, four hundred dollars!".[2] One of the two servers earning a tip from the group that evening, Ryan Brandt, covered her mouth as the surprise soaked in, and tears streamed down her face. The announcement was recorded and subsequently posted to Instagram.[3]

As Wise and the rest of his group exited the restaurant, Brandt followed them outside. "I was told that I was going to be giving my cash over to my shift manager, and I would be taking home 20%," she told Wise.[4] The news was inconsistent with Wise's intention in leaving the $4,400 tip. Having dined at the restaurant several times before, he had called ahead to specifically request Brandt as the server. Wise also asked how tips were shared at Oven & Tap to "ensure his plan wouldn't run afoul of the restaurant's tipping policy".[5] Wise understood Brandt would split the tip with the server working alongside her that

DOI: 10.4324/9781003280040-15

night, but he did not expect her to end up with a mere 20%. Hearing the news from Brandt, Wise turned around and went back inside the restaurant to speak with the manager and make the group's intentions known.

## Industry Background

As part of the leisure and hospitality industry, Oven & Tap was included in the food services and drinking places subsector of establishments that prepared food and beverages for immediate consumption (Bureau of Labor Statistics). Workers in this industry were often subjected to specific compensation practices for "tipped" employees (Exhibit 10.1). Many times, this included a policy that any tips received must be "pooled" or shared among cooks, dishwashers, and other back-of-house workers.[6] In 2020, the restaurant industry entered an "economic free fall" as the result of lockdowns, capacity restrictions, and other mandates to slow the spread of the COVID-19 virus that had become a global pandemic.[7] That year, total sales in the industry were down $240 billion.[8] By the end of 2020, 17% of all restaurants would permanently close their doors.[9]

By mid-2021, restaurants were on the path to recovery. Though all 50 states had some level of indoor dining restrictions during the previous year, industry sales were projected to increase 20% as 39 states lifted all restrictions on indoor dining.[10] Simultaneously, the industry remained one million jobs short of pre-pandemic staffing levels (Exhibit 10.2). By September 2021, leisure and hospitality employees were quitting at a rate of 6.4%, which was more than double the average 3.0% quit rate across all private sector industries (Bureau of Labour Statistics, 2021).

## Company History

Oven & Tap joined the "vibrant restaurant scene" in Bentonville, Arkansas, in 2015.[11] Co-owners Luke Wetzel and Mollie Mullis opened the modern-rustic, sit-in restaurant just outside Bentonville's downtown square.[12] The town of 54,000 was home to Walmart's headquarters, making Bentonville a "community of choice" within the broader northwest Arkansas area.[13] Oven & Tap's website invited diners to stop by for *"delicious dishes inspired by southern fare & hints of Italian flair ... [made] from scratch using house recipes & quality ingredients"*.[14] *Food Network* rated the restaurant as one of the top food destinations in Bentonville,[15] while local dining guides included Oven & Tap in their top 10 places to dine in the city.[16]

## The $100 Dinner Club

The practise of leaving large tips for service staff during the holiday season was nothing new, but in recent years the practice became a viral phenomenon. The idea behind the challenge was simple: "[Get] a group of friends together during the holidays for dinner. At the end of the meal, each person pays their share and leaves an additional $100 bill, resulting in a massive tip for the waitress and restaurant staff".[17] The so-called "$100 Dollar Dinner Club" saw a resurgence amid the pandemic as local Facebook groups for the dining clubs appeared nationwide. For example, members of the Denver $100 Dinner Club left a $3,000 tip that was split among 24 service staff.[18] In Ohio, the "Breakfast Santas" left a $3,000 tip, while a group in Virginia left $1,900.[19] "*You'd be surprised how big of impact you can [have] on someone else's life,*" noted one patron.[20]

## The Firing

When Brandt told Wise that she would not be receiving her full share of the tip on the evening of December 2, Wise walked back into Oven & Tap. He approached Wetzel and Mullis and explained that the group had *"intended to only tip the servers who'd waited on them"*.[21] Wise noted that the owners returned the tip to him, and that he handed the $2,200 directly to Brandt once outside.

On December 7th, the feel-good story of the holiday season turned sour. Local news outlets began reporting that Brandt had been terminated. As part of that news coverage, Brandt claimed, "*They fired me from Oven & Tap over the phone and I've been there for 3.5 years and that was really heartbreaking*".[22] According to Brandt, she had been terminated for communicating the company's tip sharing policy to Wise.[23] That same day, Wise launched the GoFundMe campaign to support Brandt in paying rent and buying groceries during her period of unemployment. The campaign quickly exceeded its goal, raising $8,700 for Brandt over the course of a few days.[24]

Wetzel and Mullis disputed Brandt's claim. The co-owners of Oven & Tap released an official statement three days later:[25]

> We commend the organisation that dined with us and generously gave to our staff. They have an absolute right to tip whoever they want, and we honoured that request. Oven & Tap doesn't deliver terminations lightly. Because we value our employees and highly respect their privacy, we never discuss personnel issues. The server who was terminated several days after the group dined with us was not let go because she chose to keep the tip money. The other two servers who received generous tips that evening from the ... organisation – including one who also received $2,200 – are still members of our team. Oven & Tap has always been committed to providing fair and quality compensation to all members of our restaurant team. We recognise and regret that a recent incident in our restaurant could have been handled differently by reminding our team how we would be splitting any tips prior to the event; however, our policy has always been to participate in a tip pool/share with the staff. Tip sharing is a common restaurant industry practice that we follow to ensure all of our team members are adequately compensated for their hard work.

Two days after releasing the public statement, Wetzel and Mullis continued to counter the claims of both Wise and Brandt: "They (Wise) did not call ahead and ask about our tipping policy nor did they email ... We did not know walking into this experience how much money and what this generous act really looked like," the pair reported.[26] Wetzel and Mullis further claimed the tipping policy at Oven & Tap was clear: bartenders received 6% of bar sales, while kitchen staff and server assistants receive 2% and 1% of food sales, respectively.[27] Though servers at Oven & Tap were permitted to keep cash tips, Wetzel and Mullis claimed the restaurant "normally takes a cut of servers' credit card tips to divvy among other employees," while noting that tips for large parties were handled "on a case-by-case basis".[28] In the end, approximately $7,000 was paid out to the other employees working that evening because Wetzel and Mullis felt "the entire staff worked so hard that night to serve a large party".[29]

Brandt disputed the claims made by Wetzel and Mullis. She noted the payouts for bar and kitchen staff were usually deducted from the servers' paychecks, not their tips.[30] In her 3.5 years at Oven & Tap, Brandt claimed she *"only ever split tips evenly with the servers which actually worked the function"*.[31] In response to Brandt's counterclaims, Wetzel and Mullis issued a cease-and-desist letter through their attorney. The letter alleged that Brandt had caused permanent damage to Oven & Tap's reputation through the "countless unwarranted 1 Star Reviews" that have caused Oven & Tap to now be "cast as a restaurant that treats its employees poorly".[32]

## Public Backlash

Despite the negative publicity, Wetzel and Mullis stood firm. The co-owners insisted tip sharing had always been the policy at Oven & Tap, though they noted that things *"could have been handled differently by reminding our team how we would be splitting any tips prior to the event"* (CBS News, 2021). The acknowledgement from Wetzel and Mullis made little difference as the court of public opinion continued to unleash its verdict. What is a "fair" tipping policy, and how should it be communicated? Wetzel and Mullis found themselves with many questions and few answers as they continued to navigate the onslaught of negative reviews and viral coverage of the situation.

### Discussion Questions

1 Using equity theory, evaluate the fairness of tip-sharing from the perspective of Wise, Wetzel/Mullis, and Brandt.
2 Assume Brandt agreed to take the 20% ($440) offered by her employer that evening even though she believed she deserved the full amount ($2,200). Continuing to use equity theory as a basis for evaluation, list and analyse the potential responses Brandt may have had to the inequity she perceived. How would you respond if you were in Brandt's position? Why?
3 Create a fair tip-sharing policy and procedure to address the pay equity concerns at Oven & Tap and provide recommendations to Wetzel and Mullis on how to communicate this policy effectively.

### Learning Activity: Multimedia clips

Because the situation outlined in the case actively played out over social media, there are several multimedia clips that support the case as follows:

"$10,000 Tip Left for Servers" (4'01").

This video provides a brief overview of the concept behind the $100 Dinner Club, with reactions from several servers who have benefited from the practice: https://www.youtube.com/watch?v=hbojNNP7-tM

Local news coverage – "Bentonville waitress fired days after receiving large tip" (2'24"). Local coverage of the controversy, including an interview with Brandt before she retained legal counsel: https://www.youtube.com/watch?v=oVtcMDKYCDA

National news coverage – "Arkansas Server Fired After $4,400 Tip Dispute" (3'03"). Includes interviews with Brandt, Wetzel, and Mullis: https://www.youtube.com/watch?v=UzqSXgo6ymw

Consider how the media reported on this case, and analyse and explain what you heard or read.

## Notes


1 Grant Wise. (2021, December 7). *GFM tip story* [Video]. YouTube. Available at: https://www.youtube.com/watch?v=f7WU2TDDdjY&t=13s

2 Wilson, M. (2021, December 7). *Pay it Forward: Bentonville Restaurant Workers Receive over $4,000 Tip.* 5NewsOnline. Retrieved December 13, 2021, from https://www.5newsonline.com/article/news/community/pay-it-forward-bentonville-restaurant-workers-receive-over-4000-tip-at-oven-and-tap-restaurant/527-64daf143-a881-4a8f-8a08-bec733b646b0

3 O'Kane, C. (2021, December 14). *This waitress was given a $2,200 tip. She was told she had to share it with other staff – then was fired.* CBS News. Available at: https://www.cbsnews.com/news/oven-and-tap-tip-ryan-brandt-fired/

4 Moclair, W. (2021a, December 10). *Oven & Tap Employee Let Go over $4,400 Tip.* NWAHomepage. Retrieved July 28, 2022, from https://www.nwahomepage.com/news/oven-and-tap-let-go-after-4200-tip/

5 Edwards, J. (2021, December 14). An Arkansas waitress served a party that tipped $4,400. It led to her getting fired. *The Washington Post.* Available at: https://www.washingtonpost.com/nation/2021/12/14/waitress-fired-big-tip/

6 Bureau of Labor Statistics. (2021, November 22). *Quits rate 6.6 percent in accommodation and food services in September 2021.* TED: The economics daily. Available at: https://www.bls.gov/opub/ted/2021/quits-rate-6-6-percent-in-accommodation-and-food-services-in-september-2021.htm

7 Kennedy, S. (2020, December 7). [National Restaurant Association's Letter to Congress]. Retrieved December 23, 2021, from https://restaurant.org/nra/media/downloads/pdfs/advocacy/nat-l-restaurant-assoc-ltr-to-congress-12-7-2020.pdf

8 National Restaurant Association. (n.d.). *Restaurant Industry Facts at a Glance.* Retrieved December 17, 2021, from https://restaurant.org/research-and-media/research/industry-statistics/national-statistics/

9 Kennedy, S. (2020, December 7). [National Restaurant Association's Letter to Congress]. Retrieved December 23, 2021, from https://restaurant.org/nra/media/downloads/pdfs/advocacy/nat-l-restaurant-assoc-ltr-to-congress-12-7-2020.pdf

10 National Restaurant Association. (2021, August 31). *Mid-year State of the Restaurant Industry Update.* Retrieved December 23, 2021, from https://go.restaurant.org/rs/078-ZLA-461/images/2021-SOI_Mid-Year%20Update%20Final.pdf

11 Cherry, S. (2016, October 30). Foodies flock to restaurant scene in Bentonville, Arkansas. *Tulsa World.* Available at: https://tulsaworld.com/entertainment/dining/foodies-flock-to-restaurant-scene in bentonville-arkansas/article_47a7f39e-d476-5e0c-a263-fa38bbf4c1b9.html

12 Berneking, E., Pollock Estes, K., Marthis, R., & Waszczuck, S. (2015, October). Dining day trips. *417 Magazine.* Available at: https://www.417mag.com/issues/october-2015/dining-day-trips/

13 City of Bentonville, Arkansas. (n.d.). *About Bentonville: Demographics.* Retrieved January 4, 2022, from https://www.bentonvillear.com/484/About-Bentonville

14 Oven & Tap. (n.d.). [Company website: Home tab]. Retrieved January 4, 2022, from https://www.ovenandtap.com/oven-tap

15 Robinson, K. (2021, November 7). *Where to Eat in Bentonville, Arkansas.* Food Network. Retrieved January 13, 2022, from https://www.foodnetwork.com/restaurants/photos/restaurant-guide-bentonville

16 NWAGuru. (2021, November 7). *Top 10 restaurants in Bentonville, Arkansas.* NWArkansastravelguide.com. Available at: https://nwatravelguide.com/top-10-best-restaurants-bentonville-arkansas/

17 Heggeness, G. (2019, December 13). *The '$100 diner challenge' is trending and it's a great way to give back during the holidays.* PureWow. Available at: https://www.purewow.com/wellness/100-dollar-diner-challenge
18 The Denver Channel. (2021, April 6). *Facebook group surprises Colorado restaurant staff with $3,000 in tips.* Available at: https://www.simplemost.com/facebook-group-gives-restaurant-staff-3000/
19 Roche, D. (2021, December 18). Secret 'Santa' groups are tipping waiters up to $3,000 for Christmas 2021. *Newsweek.* Available at: https://www.newsweek.com/secret-santa-groups-tipping-waiters-3000-christmas-2021-1660871
20 Wilson, M. (2021, December 7). *Pay it Forward: Bentonville Restaurant Workers Receive over $4,000 Tip.* 5NewsOnline. Retrieved December 13, 2021, from https://www.5newsonline.com/article/news/community/pay-it-forward-bentonville-restaurant-workers-receive-over-4000-tip-at-oven-and-tap-restaurant/527-64daf143-a881-4a8f-8a08-bec733b646b0
21 Edwards, J. (2021, December 14). An Arkansas waitress served a party that tipped $4,400. It led to her getting fired. *The Washington Post.* Available at: https://www.washingtonpost.com/nation/2021/12/14/waitress-fired-big-tip/
22 O'Kane, C. (2021, December 14). *This waitress was given a $2,200 tip. She was told she had to share it with other staff – then was fired.* CBS News. Available at: https://www.cbsnews.com/news/oven-and-tap-tip-ryan-brandt-fired/
23 Edwards, J. (2021, December 14). An Arkansas waitress served a party that tipped $4,400. It led to her getting fired. *The Washington Post.* Available at: https://www.washingtonpost.com/nation/2021/12/14/waitress-fired-big-tip/
24 ibid.
25 Moclair, W. (2021a, December 10). *Oven & Tap Employee Let Go over $4,400 Tip.* NWAHomepage. Retrieved July 28, 2022, from https://www.nwahomepage.com/news/oven-and-tap-let-go-after-4200-tip/
26 Moclair, W. (2021b, December 13). *Oven and Tap Owners Respond to the Server Let Go after $4,440 Tip.* NWAHomepage. Retrieved December 13, 2021, from https://www.nwahomepage.com/news/oven-and-tap-owners-respond-to-the-server-let-go-after-4400-tip/
27 ibid.
28 Edwards, J. (2021, December 14). An Arkansas waitress served a party that tipped $4,400. It led to her getting fired. *The Washington Post.* Available at: https://www.washingtonpost.com/nation/2021/12/14/waitress-fired-big-tip/
29 ibid.
30 Moclair, W. (2021c, December 14). *Restaurant Owners Respond to Backlash after Firing Server Who Got $4,400 Tip.* NWAHomepage. Retrieved July 28, 2022, from https://www.wfla.com/news/viral-news/restaurant-owners-respond-to-backlash-after-firing-server-who-got-4400-tip/
31 ibid.
32 Edwards, J. (2021, December 14). An Arkansas waitress served a party that tipped $4,400. It led to her getting fired. *The Washington Post.* Available at: https://www.washingtonpost.com/nation/2021/12/14/waitress-fired-big-tip/

## References and Suggested Reading

An overview of updated tip sharing protections enacted by the Department of Labour in 2020 and 2021: "Tip regulations under the fair labor standards act". Available at: https://www.dol.gov/agencies/whd/flsa/tips

An example of the consequences of poor tip sharing policy.

U.S. Department of Labor finds Pittsburgh restaurant illegally shared workers' tips with managers, other non-tipped employees, recovers $41k for 12 workers. Available at: https://www.dol.gov/newsroom/releases/whd/whd20211201

A YouTube video of Grant Wise telling the tip sharing story in his own words.

GFM tip story (n.d.) [Video file]. YouTube. Available at: https://www.youtube.com/watch?v=f7WU2TDDdjY&t=13s

## Exhibits

**Exhibit 10.1** Excerpt from U.S. Department of Labor's "Tip Regulations under the Fair Labor Standards Act (FLSA)"

In 2020 and 2021, the Department completed a series of rulemakings to update its regulations to protect tipped workers. These rulemakings addressed 2018 legislative amendments to section 3(m) and other sections of the Fair Labor Standards Act (FLSA) to expressly prohibit employers, including managers and supervisors, from keeping employees' tips. The rulemakings also updated the Department's "dual jobs" regulations addressing the circumstances under which an employer can take a partial credit against its minimum wage obligations based on the tips received by employees.

The current regulations were adopted through the following three rulemakings:

1 The Department published a final rule, "Tip Regulations Under the Fair Labor Standards Act (FLSA)" (2020 Tip final rule), on December 30, 2020, (See 85 FR 86756). The parts of this rule which became effective on April 30, 2021 provide:

- an employer cannot keep employees' tips under any circumstances; managers and supervisors also may not keep tips received by employees, including through tip pools;
- an employer that pays the full minimum wage and takes no tip credit may allow employees who are not tipped employees (for example, cooks and dishwashers) to participate in the tip pool;
- an employer that collects tips to facilitate a mandatory tip pool generally must fully redistribute the tips within the pay period; and,
- employers that do not take a tip credit but collect employees' tips to operate a mandatory tip pool, must maintain and preserve payroll or other records containing information on each employee who receive tips and the weekly or monthly amount reported by the employee, to the employer, of tips received.

Source: U.S. Department of Labor, Wage and Hour Division. (n.d.). Tip regulations under the Fair Labor Standards Act (FLSA). Retrieved December 16, 2022 from https://www.dol.gov/agencies/whd/flsa/tips.

**EXHIBIT 10.2** Total Employment, Eating and Drinking Places

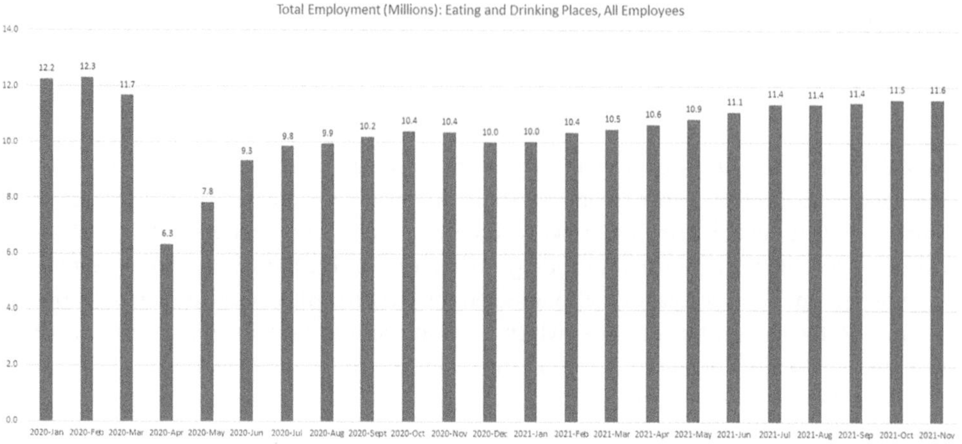


Source: Created by the authors using Bureau of Labour Statistics data retrieved December 23, 2021, from https://data.bls.gov/timeseries/CES7072200001.

# CASE 11

## STREET FOOD IN HO CHI MINH CITY

### Managing High Demand

*Khanh Le and Gillian Dixon*

**Synopsis**

Thien Tran opened Shaanxi Bao, a street food restaurant offering take-out-only buns in Ho Chi Minh City, Vietnam. By the end of August, there was a constant line-up in front of the restaurant for both online and direct food orders. Each customer had to wait for at least 25–30 minutes before reaching the front of the line. The crowds were affecting the neighbouring businesses, who had started to complain about Shaanxi's Bao customers taking over the street and parking spots. The limited space restricted Tran from setting up more food preparation workstations. The opening plan goal to create a unique customer service experience was not fully delivered, and Tran was concerned.

Thien Tran opened his first street food restaurant, Shaanxi Bao on July 30, 2019, in Ho Chi Minh City, Vietnam. On August 30, 2019, only four weeks after opening Shaanxi Bao, Tran looked at the long line of direct customers and food delivery drivers that waited for service. The street food restaurant specialised in a take-out bun with a range of topping choices. With a Chinese-food twist, the concept was like a banh mi sandwich, the French-Vietnamese hybrid made with a fluffy French baguette. While the sales targets were met daily, the lengthy wait time for both groups of customers bothered Tran, as it diminished the service focus he had established for the restaurant, speedy yet friendly service to each customer. Tran had received concerns from unhappy customers and neighbouring restaurants regarding overcrowding, and this had pushed Tran to re-evaluate his way of managing direct and online sales. One evening after a busy day, Tran commented to his partner Hoa, who was currently managing most shifts at Shaanxi Bao, "*How can I better manage these two groups of customers to improve my operation?*"

DOI: 10.4324/9781003280040-16

## Street Food in Vietnam

Street food in Vietnam was a way of life, an embedded part of Vietnam's culture and social fabric. In Ho Chi Minh City, known in Vietnam as a city that doesn't sleep, street food could be found anywhere and anytime. In 2018, Ho Chi Minh City was named by the U.S. news network as one of the 23 best street food cities in the world[1]. One year later, the city "was the supporting pillar in Vietnam and had been awarded the title of "Asia's Leading Culinary Destination," by World Travel Awards[2]". In the hustle and bustle of this city, street food was quick, inexpensive, and easy to find.

Street food in Ho Chi Minh City was not limited to a specific group of customers. Despite the low price, street food was not restricted to lower-income workers or younger students with limited budgets. In Ho Chi Minh City, street food was a part of the local culture. In this busy city, rather than frequently cooking, the tradition was to go out for street food with co-workers or friends. Street food was consumed during lunch breaks, as grab-and-go street food on the way home, or as a treat for families on the weekend. Every night around dinner time, it was normal to see big groups of friends sitting at a small table on the pavement eating and chatting. A series of food carts and small restaurants were typically on the same street. The high demand for street food resulted in a variety of options for customers as well as intense competition. For business owners in a competitive market, customers could easily choose another dish over your menu or go to another restaurant that was newer or had promotions.

The intense competition was similar for food delivery services. Getting food delivered daily was easy and normal to everyone in Ho Chi Minh City. Customers did not mind paying a VND 15,000–35,000 (USD $.61–$1.41) flat-rate service fee to the food delivery app for their food to be delivered, especially for lunch break at work, or a late-night food craved from home. There were at least seven apps to choose from that included GrabFood, GoFood, Baemin, Foody, and UberEats. Because of the competitiveness in this market, these apps differentiated themselves through their content. Some chose to focus on tucked-away street food carts or very high-end options; some provided detailed reviews to help customers choose what they liked; some simply offered promotions to sway customers. However, regardless of their unique selling points, they all considered coverage an important factor. The more restaurants and food options customers could find on one platform, the more likely they would stay and spend money on that platform. For this reason, many apps wanted to have popular restaurants on their platforms. Tran learned this insight after years of working in the restaurant industry, and he turned it into Shaanxi Bao's advantage, and, at the same time, he had created the current challenge managing high demand.

## From Nightlife to a Street-Food Restaurant

Tran was a mixologist and had been in the food & beverage industry for more than six years. His day-to-day work revolved around the bar, from creating a cocktail list to setting up a new bar and bringing it to life. He called himself a perfectionist. For that reason, even though he enjoyed every moment of the process, he admitted that setting up bars was never his biggest interest. He always felt like staying longer after opening to ensure operations and sales were stable before moving on, and, sometimes, that exhausted him. Therefore, he only agreed to take on a new project when he could see a shared passion from the investors. His goal was to be an expert in food, especially street food, and drinks. This special interest was the impetus for his street food business, Shaanxi Bao. Prior to opening Shaanxi Bao, Tran had commented:

> I have always been drawn to the art of cooking in street foods. Many of my new cocktails are inspired by street foods. I enjoy watching people make food on the street because they spark ideas in me.

As Tran spent most of his career with bars and nightlife, he wanted to bring this experience into the new business as well. From observation, he noticed that customers had developed a high expectation for excellent customer service, and the demand would only continue to grow. Tran passionately shared his insight:

> Customers want to be put at the centre and receive good service. Street food is more on the casual side, but genuine and friendly service must still be at the centre.

Before deciding to open Shaanxi Bao, Tran spent a long time doing his market research called filtering. He selectively brought street foods into the bars by pairing them with his new drinks. By directly testing the products, he knew which dishes needed improvement and which ones were easily enjoyed by customers. Based on research and observation, the time he chose to open his restaurant was when customers actively sought new cuisine and food experiences. It was also trendy for chefs or bartenders from high-end restaurants and hotels to open their own businesses. These businesses were normally street food restaurants offering simple yet appetising dishes.

Before settling down with the Shaanxi bun idea, Tran had also researched the viability of different street foods around the world. He found that Chinese food had always had a solid place in many countries, and Vietnam was no exception. Therefore, picking a Chinese fusion dish appeared to be a guaranteed win for him. Tran chose to stay simple and stick with only one dish (with multiple choices of protein) to ensure he could provide speedy service, one of the key expectations for street food in Vietnam (Exhibit 11.1). Tran commented to a colleague:

> At Shaanxi Bao, customers will get to try the authentic flavour – the taste they expect when travelling abroad. I'm bringing that flavour to them here at a street-food price range. I just have to sell more to cover the high cost of quality ingredients.

The name Shaanxi Bao was also intentional. Most restaurant names were after the trend of "Mrs. (owner's name)." Tran chose Shaanxi Bao because the only dish here came from this province of China, so customers could easily imagine the style of the food as soon as they heard the name. Customers could call it Shaanxi Bao or Bao Shaanxi without messing up the meaning. Since this inventive name style was not popular at the time, Tran called Shaanxi Bao a rule-breaking innovation.

From ideas to the ready-to-serve restaurant, Tran did not actively consult any expert in the industry. As Tran was the sole investor and owner of this business, he made all the decisions without having a second opinion. He found using his own money for his investment had removed the pressure of paying monthly interest, and any time-consuming discussions for every decision. He believed that a successful start-up was a combination of a well-developed concept and prompt execution. Tran had seen many ideas that were never brought to life because of mixed opinions from different experts. Tran never thought that having different perspectives was excessive; he simply did not find it necessary for this project. The words "execution" and "passionate" were repeated multiple times when Tran talked about bringing ideas to life.

## From Popularity to Crowdedness

When searching for a location, Tran had stuck to his vision and intentionally avoided the main, crowded streets, where many branded or big restaurants were located. This kind of location served two purposes, it minimised competition with well-established restaurants and responded to a new food trend in which foodies often looked for off-the-beaten-path experiences. Foodies were customers who were more willing to try new dishes as well as to enjoy them and share with other people. Shaanxi Bao could, then, benefit from word-of-mouth marketing. Everything was running well until, at the end of August, Tran noticed some problems starting that related to high volume.

> I did not expect Shaanxi Bao to get so popular and crowded so quickly. Of course, I want it to be busy with all the research and investment that I put in, but the number of customers and orders within two weeks of opening caught me off guard a little bit. Customers are waiting an hour before the restaurant opens.

Shaanxi Bao's busy crowd consisted of both direct customers and food-delivery drivers who picked up online orders. These drivers were from three different platforms that Tran had registered with: GrabFood, Foody, and Baemin. The pricing was similar for both direct and online customers. No special promotions were offered to both groups. Tran did not have to pay any commission to the food delivery services because these companies proactively approached him to put ads of Shaanxi Bao on their apps. At first, he refused to have these delivery apps advertise Shaanxi Bao; however, after negotiations, he agreed to work with these apps on a non-commission basis, if they published the correct information, images, and pricing provided by him. The popularity of Shaanxi Bao attracted these food-delivery platforms even with the customer-paid service fee and minimum vendor fee negotiated by Tran.

In Tran's original plan, the direct customer was the main target market, especially with the service he aimed to provide. However, towards the end of the first busy month, he noticed that the ratio for direct customers and online platforms was around 55–45. Tran managed to have two separate lines for each group, but most customers still had to wait between 20–30 minutes to receive their orders. The wait sometimes was beyond 30 minutes during rush hour. The rush for online started around 3 pm and came mostly from people working in offices. The general rush hours were between 4–5 pm. and 8–9 pm. At times, he had to close online orders to handle the customers in front of him.

> I just don't want to take so many online orders and then inform them that I am out of buns. If customers keep getting that 'out of stock' message too many times, they will not want to come back.

Tran liked the online order market because it was more stable. Food delivery was available around the clock whether it was raining or steaming hot outside; they helped Shaanxi Bao reach customers who lived far away. Tran also mentioned that online orders gave him a consistent number of orders and revenue daily, especially when the apps ran promotions. These promotions were offered by the apps and had not affected Shaanxi's Bao costs.

As a cash business, like many other businesses in Vietnam, Tran did not have any sales reports to know which customer stream brought him more money. However, he believed that direct customers brought him more value. Whenever customers visited Shaanxi Bao, they would receive the great service that Tran trained his staff to provide. Moreover, they got to taste the hot bun when it was at its best. Once they enjoyed the food and the experience, they would share the experience with friends, families, on social media, and Shaanxi Bao benefited from free marketing. Compared to online orders, the quality of food for direct orders was more consistent. With online orders, food delivery sometimes ran multiple orders from multiple locations for different customers. Customers sometimes received soggy or cold buns. They also missed out on the instruction on how to enjoy the bun with the perfect sauce. As a result, bad reviews had started to appear on different apps.

Besides the quality concerns, the neighbouring business owners in the same food and beverage industry reacted in an unfriendly manner when too many customers waited around for Shaanxi Bao, especially when parking spots were limited in the small street where Shaanxi Bao was located (Exhibit 11.2). The neighbouring businesses would tell Tran's customers not to cross certain areas when parking. Tran could see how unfriendly they were towards him and his customers. Some businesses had chosen to file complaints with the local authority as well.

Shaanxi Bao also had some internal concerns. Since Tran had wanted to limit risk, he had opened with limited staff and equipment. When the restaurant got busier, there was not enough space to set up more workstations and equipment to speed up the assembly steps, and the line could not move fast enough. The number of buns sold per day was capped at around 400–450 buns. There were two kinds of reactions from customers; some thought of Shaanxi Bao as the must-try trending food or the "hype"; some were disappointed having to wait in the long line to find out that they had limited to no options. Tran explained this supply issue was related to a small kitchen.

> From a marketing viewpoint, the hype is such a great way to get customers excited about our buns. But, partially, the real reason to limit buns sold is our scale. We do not have a big kitchen; all ingredients are prepared in the back and assembled at the front.

From the employee side, they had to work under a lot of pressure when the restaurant was constantly busy, to keep up with orders, line ups, and the provision of good service (Exhibit 11.3). Sometimes, it was so busy that the employees skipped breaks. Tran required employees to treat all customers equally and politely. No matter how long the line was, customers should feel that they were listened to and cared for. Whenever customers had comments on the food or service, the team would take notes and show appreciation for the feedback. Tran believed that in addition to the food, the service was a key selling point.

Tran knew that he needed to re-evaluate his business model. Shaanxi Bao could not provide the speedy service he needed. Tran was concerned that his initial plans had compromised customer service for direct customers and the food quality for online orders. In the long term, these issues could damage sales for both delivery channels. Tran was also concerned about upsetting the neighbouring businesses and overworking his team. Tran had his sights on expansion, but first, he needed to revisit his food distribution strategy for Shaanxi Bao.

**Discussion Question**

1 What are the strengths and weaknesses of Tran's current business approach?
2 What are the operational needs for the two different food distribution systems at Shaanxi Bao?
3 If Tran were to choose a target market – online or direct customers – which market should he choose and why?
4 What can be changed to the food distribution system to reduce customer wait times and manage expectations?

**Learning Activity: Online Food Delivery and Impacts on Sustainability**

Li, C., Mirosa, M., & Bremer, P. (2020). Review of online food delivery platforms and their impacts on sustainability. *Sustainability, 12*(14), 5528.

Read the article "Review of Online Food Deliver Platforms and their Impacts on Sustainability" by Mirosa and Bremer (2020). Based on the reading and your experience as either a customer, or a food delivery provider, consider and discuss your responses together to the following questions.

1 Name some of the economic impacts related to food delivery and then discuss their significance (pros and cons).
2 Name some of the social impacts that you have noticed related to food delivery and then discuss what can be learned from these impacts.
3 Name some of the environmental impacts that you have noticed related to food delivery and then discuss what can be done to minimise them.

## Notes

1 Movida. (2023). *Movida: About*. Retrieved April 26, 2023, from https://www.movida.com.au/about/
2 Nguyen, S. V. (2021, August 01). *Ho Chi Minh city goes global: World-class street food as centerpiece*. Tuoi Tre News.

## References and Further Reading

Best Ever Food Review Show. (2022). Saigon hidden noodle tour!! Must try before you die!! [Video file]. YouTube. Available at: https://www.youtube.com/watch?v=B2PLVAxl3Fw

Li, C., Mirosa, M., & Bremer, P. (2020). Review of online food delivery platforms and their impacts on sustainability. *Sustainability, 12*(14), 5528.

Nguyen, S. V. (2021, August 1). *Ho Chi Minh city goes global: World-class street food as centerpiece*. Tuoi Tre News.

## Exhibits

**Exhibit 11.1** Bao Bun with Various Toppings

Source: Photo by marta filipczyk on unsplash.

**Exhibit 11.2** Food Delivery Drivers and Direct Customers Waiting in Front of the Restaurant to Pick up Online Orders

Source: Author's own.

**Exhibit 11.3** A View of Shaanxi Bao from the Street

Source: Author's own.

# CASE 12

## A STORY OF RESILIENCE AT THE RESTAURANT COMIDA CORRIDA

*Sandra Cherro Osorio and Esha Thukral*

**Synopsis**

In November 2020, Frank Camorra proudly opened Tres a Cinco, located at the former site of Camorra's late night Spanish-inspired bodega Bar Tini, and next to Movida Original and Movida Aqui at Hosier Lane in Melbourne's central business district. Camorra had appointed Chef Sarai Castillo as Head Chef, and Castillo had retained the staff that had worked with her during the pandemic. This was a success story for Camorra and Castillo, one that told the story of resilience, and it was a story they both wanted to share with other businesses and employees.

### Frank Camorra and the Movida Group

Frank Camorra opened his first restaurant Movida Original in 2002. The concept was developed around a celebration of Spanish produce, culinary techniques, and traditions. Two more two restaurants followed with Movida Next Door in 2008, and Movida Aqui in 2009. In 2018 the Movida group also added Movida Lorne.[1] The food was traditionally Spanish, and the restaurants were highly popular among Melbournians and visitors to the state of Victoria.

When the pandemic started in 2020, the Australian government imposed a national lockdown on March 28 to curb the transmission of COVID-19. Businesses of all sizes were affected by this measure, and the impact was profound on small- to medium-sized enterprises (SMEs) as they experienced greater challenges due to their size and often limited financial resources. The lockdown forced restaurants to close their doors and think of ways to continue their business, but more importantly, retain staff for as long as closures took place. To support the businesses during the lockdowns, the Australian government announced several measures, including investment impetus through depreciation deductions, increasing the asset write-off threshold, a credit guarantee scheme for SMEs, and tax subsidies to help businesses hibernate until the virus was contained or at least until it was safe to operate again.[2] The Australian government also introduced two wage supplement schemes

DOI: 10.4324/9781003280040-17

called Jobkeeper and Jobseeker.[3] Jobkeeper was set up to support eligible businesses to cover the cost of wages for their staff during the lockdowns, and the latter was for eligible people that had lost their jobs or had reduced working hours due to the lockdowns. To apply for these schemes, employees needed to meet certain criteria: be an Australian citizen, hold a permanent visa, or be a Special Category (Subclass 444) visa holder on 1 March 2020.[4] When these government response measures were announced, millions of workers on temporary visas, including international students, were excluded from the schemes and were left to look after themselves. [5]

## Chef Sarai Castillo

In March 2020, Chef Castillo was part of the staff in Movida Aqui, a restaurant that was part of the Movida Group. A Mexican-born chef, Castillo was a temporary visa holder who had lived and worked in Australia for the past seven years. For the last five years she had worked at Movida Aqui. On March 5, 2020, Movida Aqui advised Castillo that she, and some other colleagues who were on temporary visas, would have to stay home. Ineligible for any financial support from the government for employees on temporary visas, their employer, Movida Group, was unable to keep them on the payroll.

Chef Carai Castilla had no formal training on how to be a chef. On moving to Australia, she had chosen to work as a cook and to build on the skills she had developed as a home cook in Mexico. The pandemic placed Castillo in a precarious situation, and her main concern was how to continue to maintain an income. Castillo believed she had to take matters into her own hands and act for herself, and she purposefully decided to maintain an optimistic outlook. On announcement of the layoff from Movida Aqui, she started to brainstorm options to generate an income. One idea that she had early, and decided to focus on, was to prepare Mexican food from her home kitchen. Castillo's idea was to sell food in her neighbourhood. As Castillo started to develop this idea she received a call from her boss, Camorra. In a conversation with Camorra, Castillo learned that Camorra had a new idea for the restaurants. The idea was to offer home delivery of pre-packaged meals with iconic dishes previously available in the restaurants. To proceed with this plan, Chef Castillo and other colleagues were called back to the kitchen at Movida Aqui.

Castillo had previously included some Mexican-inspired starters in the menu at Movida Aqui and she had also worked as Sous Chef in Movida Lorne, a restaurant located in regional Victoria. Camorra predicted that people in lockdown would want nutritious home-style food. Camorra recognised Castillo's capabilities and cooking style, and suggested Castillo cook traditional Mexican food like "*what your family would eat at home.*" Castillo was motivated to take this on and approached the task with joy and commitment, as it was an opportunity to showcase her heritage and culinary skills. The new home delivery packages allowed Castillo to retain her job and continue to earn income. Castillo's enthusiasm and good disposition were noticed by Camorra.

## Limited Rotating Menu

For fast food and casual restaurants, the pivot to delivery mode was seamless as takeaway was already part of their operational business model. For fine dining or high-end restaurants, however, the adaption of their offering to delivery mode was challenging[6] and required them to explore different innovative practises.[7] Movida Group had no prior experience in food delivery. However, Camorra's influence and positive mindset was noticeable in his decisions to keep the business afloat and minimise any impact on employee's wellbeing. He decided to quickly adapt to the new demand and designed a menu for takeaway based on iconic Spanish dishes. In the first month, he worked alongside full-time employees who were eligible for the wage supplement scheme offered by the government called Job keeper, and some of his staff, including Castillo, on temporary visas, who needed to maintain an income were also asked to return to the kitchen. Due to the uncertainty regarding the duration of the lockdowns and to address the demand for healthy meals, Camorra diversified the menu at X. In addition to Spanish prepacked meals, he added Mexican traditional home-style cooked food for pick up in boxes. The transition was relatively smooth as the two cuisines shared basic ingredients and Camorra was also the owner of a food import business, which made accessibility to ingredients possible.

Castillo's name was the first that came to his mind as she was an exemplar employee with good attitude. Camorra trusted Castillo and provided her with full support to start the menu design process and inventory. Chef Castillo was brought onboard to curate a limited option menu with a total of six items: two options for breakfast, two for lunch, and two for dinner. The menu changed every week to avoid repetition and allow for the inclusion of different dishes. Changing the menu was a challenge because they had to keep the inventory well managed and avoid wastage. Castillo often took inspiration from what her Mexican mom would cook for her kids on a regular, day-to-day basis. When possible, Castillo would use similar ingredients to create different dishes that offered variety and kept customers happy.

In order to keep Sarai and other workers employed, the owner Frank Camorra offered her the opportunity to launch "*Comida Corrida,*" a takeaway Mexican home-style food service operating via an online platform named Providoor.

On Thursday, September 10, 2020, Castillo, together with Camorra, launched *Comida Corrida*, a special Mexican-style home food delivered in boxes that operated on an online platform. *Comida Corrida* translated to the pre-set menu of three courses traditionally offered at *fondas,* small old-fashioned eateries that were generally run by a female cook. The success of *Comida Corrida* was outstanding, so it was extended to November 2020. Castillo's food was inspired by her heritage and knowledge of traditional Mexican cuisine, but more importantly, it was a demonstration of her personal resilience towards difficulties she faced as an immigrant.

## Communication with Customers

Camorra understood that for an effective business operation, communication was key. During the pandemic customers needed to be informed of operational changes. At Movida Group, social media helped the restaurants keep their customers up to date. They posted daily specials, promotions, and updates on hours of operation, and they used social media to inform their customers about *Comida Corrida.* Through social media customers received information and announcements about the new venture entirely staffed by chefs and wait staff who were not eligible for any government support. The company thanked customers for their ongoing support while also posting regular updates about the weekly menu *Comida Corrida.* In the world of isolation and uncertainty, the social media platform established a connection with their online community. Celebrations were encouraged through food, including Mexican Independence Day held on September 16 (Exhibit 12.1).

## Employee Work Schedule and Roles

Businesses were required to conform with social distancing requirements imposed by the Australian government while meeting the new demand of their business operations, which included pivoting to take out boxes and food delivery. At the workplace, only a certain number of employees were allowed to work in a space, and they were required to wear a mask. Hence, Camorra decided to adjust the working schedule of employees and pivot their roles. In the case of *Comida Corrida*, employees were scheduled for a six-hour work shift that was rotated among all of them. Roles were also re-evaluated to keep employees engaged and employed. Employees preparing *Comida Corrida* participated in a range of roles. Chef Castillo proposed meals for approval by Camorra. She also worked with a pastry chef in planning the preparation of traditional Mexican desserts. Chefs were also in charge of vacuum-sealed meals for delivery. Wait staff packed boxes and drove vans for delivery within the limited radius of 20 kilometres from the central business district. Hosts acted as phone operators and received calls, answered inquiries, and took orders. The key was to keep a work schedule that allowed for the safety of all employees and achieve an optimum sales volume. Despite the challenges, the positive reception of *Comida Corrida* gave Camorra the business opportunity he needed.

## Introducing Tres a Cinco

Comida Corrida was so well received and appreciated by the customers that Movida Group, under Camorra's guidance, decided to give this project a permanent platform in the form of a restaurant named Tres a Cinco. Tres a Cinco was located at the former site of Camorra's late night Spanish-inspired bodega Bar Tini, next to Movida Original and Movida Aqui at Hosier Lane in Melbourne (Exhibit 12.2). The restaurant opened in November 2020, and Chef Castillo was offered the position of the Head Chef. Staff who worked with her during the pandemic also continued to work with her in this venture.

The restaurant kept some of their bestselling lockdown dishes on the menu, including Castillo's favourite childhood dishes like "*chilaquiles rojos,*" a flavour bomb of pan-fried tortilla chips doused in spicy red chilli sauce and topped with feta and a fried egg, and a most-loved childhood dessert, "*a Mexican icebox cake called lemon carlota.*" By serving a bit of everything from around Mexico, she showcased her culinary skills and love for food but also contributed to the many layers that made up multicultural Melbourne. Her journey of survival from pandemic-related adversity to being a head chef of the restaurant had taken nine months.

In November 2020, Castillo and Camorra met in a café to celebrate. They believed that their story could inspire and support other individuals and businesses to be resilient. They wanted to share what they had undergone during the pandemic. Their next step was to share lived experiences and lessons clearly with other businesses. What were the key lessons, and how should they communicate them to others?

### Discussion Questions

1 What were the changes in the external environment that made conducting regular business operations at Movida a significant challenge?

2 How did Movida adapt and pivot their business model to overcome the challenging times during the pandemic?
3 Considering Castillo and Camorra journeys, in what ways does this case profile individual resilience?
3 What are the connections between resilient individuals and resilient actions in Movida?

### Learning Activity: Reflection

Identifying and leveraging your strengths enhances resilience. Reflect on the positive traits you have and how you can make a difference using them.

Working in pairs, share your response to the following question:

What do you consider to be three positive traits that enhance your resilience?

## Notes

1 Movida. (2023). *Movida: About.* Retrieved April 26, 2023, from https://www.movida.com.au/about/
2 Cassells, R., Duncan, A., Kiely, D., & Mavisakalyan, A. (2020, July 7). *Impact and Response of Businesses in Australia to COVID-19.* Retrieved February 14, 2023, from https://bcec.edu.au/assets/2020/07/BCEC-COVID19-Brief-7-Business-Impact-and-Response-_final.pdf
3 Australia's Human Rights Commission. (2021). *Australia's Response to the COVID-19 Pandemic.* Retrieved February 22, 2023, from https://humanrights.gov.au/sites/default/files/2020-10/australias_response_to_the_covid-19_pandemic_-_australias_third_upr_2021.pdf
4 Australian Government: Treasury. (2020). *Economic Response to the Coronavirus.* Retrieved February 22, 2023, from https://treasury.gov.au/sites/default/files/2020-04/JobKeeper_frequently_asked_questions_2.pdf
5 Fraser, E. (2020). *The Essential Restaurant Workers the Government Forgot.* Retrieved February 22, 2023, from https://www.broadsheet.com.au/national/food-and-drink/article/watch-essential-restaurant-workers-government-forgot
6 Norris, C. L., Taylor Jr, S., & Taylor, D. C. (2021). Pivot! How the restaurant industry adapted during COVID-19 restrictions. *International Hospitality Review, 35*(2), 132–155.
7 Cherro Osorio, S. G., Delevska, A., & Matheis, P. (2021). "High-end restaurants during COVID-19: The beginning of a new fine-dining era?" In M., Sigala, R., Presbury, K. A., Smith, M., Fang, & A., Yeark (Eds.), *Case based research in tourism, travel, hospitality and events.* Singapore: Springer Nature.

## References and Suggested Reading

Hadjielias, E., Christofi, M., & Tarba, S. (2022). Contextualizing small business resilience during the COVID-19 pandemic: evidence from small business owner-managers. *Small Bus Econ, 59*(1), 1351–1380.

Shmul, Y., Reeves, M., & Levin, S. (2022). Building a mutually reinforcing system of organisational and personal resilience. BCG Henderson Institute. Retrieved April 15, 2023, from https://www.bcg.com/publications/2022/building-organizational-personal-resilience-reinforcing-system

## Exhibits

**Exhibit 12.1** Social Media Post to Commemorate Mexican Independence Day

Comida Corrida Week II - Sept 16th is Mexican Independence Day commemorating the beginning of the War of Independence which dragged on for over a decade. Typically it'd be celebrated with street parties, fireworks, the usual festivities but here in Melbourne lockdown the best we can do is a fantastic box of Mexican food delivered to your door with a couple of cocktails thrown in from our wonderful partners in this project @tequilatromba

Included in Sarai's Comida Corrida menu this week is the gorgeous 'Chiles en Nogada' pictured above. The dish relies upon mild but flavourful Poblano chili which comes into season from late August and are usually abundant by the 16th of September, in Mexico at least. The green chilies are stuffed with spiced mince, garnished with red berries and served with a white sauce of toasted almonds, creating a dish that draws on the colours of the Mexican national flag ¡Viva Mexico!

$160 including delivery. Limited allocation each week - delivered only on Thursday, 20km from the CBD. Pickup also available.

Link in bio or visit our website

Source: With permission from Movida Melbourne. Movida Melbourne. (2020). *Movida Melbourne*. Retrieved March 31, 2023, from 9https://www.facebook.com/movida.melbourne/posts/comida-corrida-week-ii-sept-16th-is-mexican-independence-day-commemorating-the-b/3467995586598267/

**Exhibit 12.2** Photograph of the Exterior of Tres a Cinco

Source: The authors.

**PART 4**

# Events and the Visitor Experience

The cases in this part share the possibilities events and visitor experiences present to attract visitation, entertain, and contribute to the local economy. Events also educate, inform and transform beyond the initial visit offering the possibility of influencing post visit behaviour.

DOI: 10.4324/9781003280040-18

# CASE 13

## GAME, SET, AND MATCH

### Increasing the Economic Impact of a Tennis Tournament in Eastbourne, England

*Nigel Jarvis*

**Synopsis**

Annie Wills was the Head of the Tourism and Leisure Department for Eastbourne, England. The Eastbourne Borough Council helped manage an annual major tennis tournament. The Council was looking for advice and suggestions to make their day tripper tennis fans stay longer and ultimately spend more money in Eastbourne. This would help to create a stronger tourism multiplier effect for Eastbourne. Any strategies should also help to inspire visitor satisfaction so that visitors would return to the destination in future years. Wills reflected on strategies that worked well in the past to encourage visitors to stay longer and wanted to explore new ideas and suggestions on how to make their day tripper tennis fans stay longer and ultimately spend more money.

The Eastbourne Borough Council helped manage a prominent annual grass court sport event that took place a week before Wimbledon, the third Grand Slam event of the season. In years past, the Council had explored ways to maximise the economic impact of day trippers to the event as well as to increase visitor satisfaction so that tennis spectators might return the following year to attend the tournament. Annie Wills, Head of the Tourism and Leisure Department for Eastbourne Borough Council, decided it was time to develop a new strategy to effectively increase the economic impact of this international tournament to the benefit of as many Eastbourne businesses as possible. This was because she realised the visitor economic impact of the event was not being maximised to its fullest potential. Wills and the Council agreed on July 4, 2022, that it was time to look to tourism and event experts for advice and suggestions on how to make their day tripper tennis fans stay longer and ultimately spend more money in the destination.

DOI: 10.4324/9781003280040-19

### Tourism in Eastbourne and the Role of Head of Tourism and Leisure

In 2013 the Council had approved a town plan, with the overall aim to ensure the town centre remained a vibrant, attractive, and welcoming place for the whole community with a strong mix of shopping, leisure, and tourism attractions together with great places to live, work and relax. The town wanted to attract a healthy number of visitors to their seaside resort throughout the year but to sustainable levels. In 2022, in addition to helping implement the tourism elements of the town plan, Wills was responsible for the operation of a range of facilities and services, such as parks and gardens, overseeing some public attractions such as the art gallery and museum, managing local theatres and leisure centres, granting film permits, and ensuring access to the seafront. Part of her duties were also to work with other nearby councils such as Lewes to help market the area on a regional basis. She had also collaborated with other local stakeholders, such as the Eastbourne Hospitality Association and Eastbourne Business Improvement District (BID), to help facilitate the tourism development strategy in the town plan.

Wills worked with about 20 key stakeholders representing the tourism and leisure sector in addition to about 100 staff in total. A key responsibility for Wills was attempting to balance the budget. Wills had commented to her trusted colleague:

> Tourism and leisure are seen as a discretionary spend whereas other Council services are statutory, meaning funds have to be spent on those services … thus I have to fight for funds for my department and this can involve some politics, depending on what people and political party were running the Council. Some political parties are more supportive of discretionary spending for tourism compared to others as they see the value of how much tourism has brought to the town … because we run our tourism and events from a commercial perspective, we do not have so much of a challenge compared to other Councils I know.

In addition, Eastbourne Borough Council helped support a portfolio of events such as the annual Airbourne airshow, which could attract up to half a million visitors over four days in August, to classic car shows and beer festivals. The Council also helped manage a prestigious annual sport event, the International Eastbourne Tennis Tournament. The grass court event traditionally took place a week before the third Grand Slam, Wimbledon in London.

### Annie Wills, Head of Tourism and Leisure, Eastbourne, UK

Wills was the Head of the Tourism and Leisure Department for Eastbourne Borough Council in southeast England, a coastal resort destination with a population of just over 100,000, according to 2021 UK Census data. Having grown up in the town and with interests in journalism and business, Wills had applied for a job to work as an accommodation booking officer at the local tourist information centre in 2000. Within two weeks she was promoted to managing the centre and thus quickly learned to network closely with a range of attraction, hotel, and restaurant stakeholders. She worked alongside the former Head of Tourism and Leisure, and when he left his post in 2009, she had applied for the job since she was familiar with so many of the required duties. Reflecting on her job in 2022, Wills said *"the thing I enjoy most about being Head is the satisfaction of delivering an event and the joy when one was finished … I never become tired of that. I also really enjoy hearing about visitor's satisfaction once they come to Eastbourne."*

## Increasing the Economic Impacts of Tourism in Eastbourne

In July 2022, Wills was very busy with her day-to-day operations, and she and her small management team had little time to undertake primary research on tourist or event visitors for any number of projects. One pressing issue in which she was particularly interested was how to increase the economic spend of visitors. According to statistics promoted by the Council, Eastbourne attracted about 4.9 million people annually, who spent about £290 million, for an average visitor expenditure of £60 per person. Wills said the latest figures from 2022 showed tourism was worth about 29% of Eastbourne's Gross Domestic Product (GDP), significantly more than the 2019 pre-pandemic levels figure of 10.3% for the United Kingdom as a whole.[1] This was not surprising for a resort town whose main industry is tourism. Wills said this was illustrated further by the sector supporting 7,000 full- and part-time equivalent jobs. Approximately 45% of all visitors to the destination were day visitors who had a much lower spend compared to overnight travellers. The resort town has a reputation of attracting an older clientele, but Wills contended this was a bit outdated and in fact many younger adults, as well as young families, were attracted to not only the coast and beach, but also its portfolio of events and attractions. However, Wills admitted the legacy of her town being a place that appealed to a stereotypical older visitor was difficult to escape and may have affected some visitors from ever going to the destination.

A recent study by the Council showed 1 in 5 people visiting the town had never been before. Wills was adamant that when people visited her town they were pleasantly surprised by the place, turning around their somewhat negative destination image so that they were more inclined to visit in the future. Wills believed attracting first-time visitors by the destination's appealing newer events geared toward younger people, along with some of their longstanding events, like their annual tennis tournament, generated repeat and loyal visitors. This was important for destination management organisations as it was 6–7% more costly to acquire new customers or visitors compared to existing ones.[2]

Visit Britain (2022), the body that markets the country to both international and domestic visitors, indicated that the typical tourist spent £39 per day visit in the United Kingdom, while for leisure trips it was somewhat less at £31. The daily expenditure could increase by four times to about £160 per day when visitors stayed overnight. This additional expenditure mainly came from eating out in local restaurants, staying in accommodation, shopping, and seeing local attractions. Hence, overnight tourists were highly prised. This was also confirmed by Wills, with similar expenditures from day trippers to Eastbourne spending three-quarters (75%) less than an overnight visitor and about 83% less than a business conference delegate. Indeed, the Council published some statistics that indicated nearly 20% of total visitor spend related to accommodation, and 35% came from food and drink. The remaining spend came from shopping, visiting other attractions, transport, and other indirect costs.

## The Economic Impacts of the International Eastbourne Tennis Tournament

The annual tennis tournament in the town was one of the major events it held, attracting a number of top female and male professional tennis players from the WTA and ATP circuits. It had been held since the 1970s and was a popular stop on the circuit. Eastbourne Borough Council provided and managed Devonshire Park (Exhibit 13.1), the grounds where the tourney took place. The Council was also responsible for the stewarding of the event. However, the day-to-day operations of the tennis tournament was left to the Lawn

Tennis Association (LTA), the national governing body for tennis in Great Britain. Players enjoyed the small, intimate nature of the town and its tennis facilities. Most players were seen about town in local restaurants and coffee shops and were very accessible compared to other well-known larger tournaments.

The week-long event in mid to late June attracted significant television coverage within the country, but also was shown overseas on dedicated sport and tennis channels. An LTA report given to Wills reported 2022's tournament had a television broadcast audience of 25.1 million, with 4.2 million social media impressions and 302,000 interactions on LTA channels. Wills stated the television images were *"great ... we cannot afford to buy PR like that. It is all free."* Television coverage worked well when the weather was sunny, but a negative view could be created if the conditions were less than ideal, such as wind and rain, for which Eastbourne could also be known. Past champions included legendary players such as Martina Navratilova and Chris Evert, to more recent winners, including Novak Djokovic, Petra Kvitová, and Taylor Fritz.

Wills was pleased that the Devonshire Park grounds had been improved in recent years with more dedicated seating on additional courts and had a maximum capacity of 55,000 for the 2023 edition of the tournament. In the past it had drawn about 40,000 tennis fans for the week, including local residents and also day trippers from either the immediate area and those within about a 90-minute drive or train journey to overnight domestic and international fans. Attendance varied depending on what players participated. In 2022, Serena Williams had announced she was playing doubles in Eastbourne after a long injury layoff, which had resulted in increased ticket sales and media coverage (Exhibits 13.2 and 13.3). The LTA provided Wills some statistics on the 2022 tournament. A total of 45,000 attended the event, with half of them being non-local. The vast majority of fans were British, with some from nearby continental countries such as France, Germany, and the Netherlands.

In 2022, like other years, most day fans arrived by train coming from Sussex, Surrey, and the greater London area. The overnight visitors tended to stay in local hotels and other types of accommodation, and the Council was very satisfied with their total spend. The LTA reported 37,500 commercial bed nights were used during the tournament. It estimated the tennis week generated just over £4 million in economic impact. Wills provided some 2022 statistics to show day trippers who visited for the tennis tournament spent £36.77, compared to overnight visitors, who spent £114.68, which was more than 3 times. Wills said the occupancy rate for accommodation was near capacity for the entire week with fans booking their places months in advance. Most spectators were middle-aged people, with an equal mix of both genders. The tournament also drew a large number of retired people. Historically, when the event was a women's-only tournament, it attracted a noticeable LGBTQ fan base, and these fans still made up a considerable share of attendees. Indeed, the LTA organised a Friday Pride Day in 2022 that focused on LGBTQ+ inclusion, with progress pride flags and hosted a group of national and local stakeholders. The LTA also coordinated a She Rallies event, to develop the female tennis workforce. The 2022 tournament was well attended by school-age children, with local primary educational institutions annually being involved in LTA Youth activities. A total of 1,650 school children engaged with tennis in the area.

The tennis tournament site was located within a 15-minute walk from the main train station (Exhibit 13.1). It was a 3- to 5-minute stroll to the seafront. Whilst the grounds were mainly located in a residential neighbourhood, there were some restaurants and a few local shops adjacent to the site. A much larger range of stores and eating establishments were located in the town centre, about a 10- to 20-minute walk from the tournament. There were limited car spaces on the site, so visitors tended to use local street parking, but this demand was high, and some visitors had to walk up to 30 minutes to find free parking. Exhibit 13.1 identifies the location of Eastbourne in the southeast of the United Kingdom, as well as neighbouring councils in East Sussex.

### Strategies to Increase the Tourism Multiplier Effect of Day Tripper Tennis Visitors

Whilst most visitors were satisfied with the event, the Council had looked at strategies to encourage tennis day trippers to spend longer at the destination. They were interested in either trying to motivate day trippers to spend at least one night in the destination or just simply to remain longer on the days of the tournament. This was ultimately to get them to spend more money by going to local restaurants and/or shopping. The Council had explored ways to maximise the economic impact of day trippers as well as increase visitor satisfaction of the event so that they may return the following year to attend the tournament. The Council were always looking for advice and suggestions on effective ways to increase the economic impact.

Wills was very well aware that longer stays in the town led to a greater tourism multiplier effect in Eastbourne. The multiplier effect was commonly used to investigate both direct and indirect expenditures in tourism and how tourism linked to other sectors in a local destination. For example, a tennis fan's direct expenditure related to attending the tournament included their travel to the event, the cost of the entrance, food and drink, and perhaps some spending at any vendors located at the tournament site. Indirect spending may include shopping off-site, perhaps on the way to or from the venue to the train station or being inspired to pay for tennis lessons post attending the event. The tourism multiplier showed the visitor initial expenditure circulating throughout the local destination's economy, either staying within the area as much as possible for a stronger effect or weakened if there existed some leakages where some spend left the local area. However, multipliers need to be carefully calculated with input from economists in conjunction with local tourism officials; otherwise, the visitor spend could be over-estimated and misused to exaggerate the value of tourism.

On a national scale, tourism's impact was amplified through the economy, so its impact was much wider than just direct spending levels.[3] Deloitte estimated the gross value added tourism multiplier in the United Kingdom to be 2.8, meaning that for every £1,000 generated through direct spending there was a further £1,800 that was supported elsewhere in the economy through supply chain and consumer spending. Nations tended to have the largest multiplier scores, normally well above 1.0 for most developed countries because of their sophisticated and strongly interlinked economies. However, as noted by Wall (1997), smaller regions and towns naturally possessed much lower multiplier figures. For example, some towns may have multipliers of only 0.35–0.50 as they cannot fully satisfy the demands of tourists, leading to leakages from the local economy. Leakages may be related to importing labour, bringing in vendors for food and shopping who may come from far away, and some people who cannot find local accommodation and have to stay quite a distance from the destination.

Eastbourne Borough Council had supplied some statistics to demonstrate the £290 million total visitor spend ultimately was estimated to worth about £400 million to the local economy, indicating the tourism multiplier effect created additional value to the town. While no multiplier estimate had ever been calculated in Eastbourne in this case, because of the considerable time and cost to determine, the figure was clearly significantly less than 1.0, in line with similar sized destinations. Further, the multiplier was rarely calculated for individual events in most destinations, instead simply relying on total visitors and overall spend for the whole year. If economic multiplier figures were ever calculated for sport tourism events, they tended to be conducted on high-profile mega-events such as the Olympics. Hence, the Council had no idea what the multiplier figure would be for their tennis tournament. Ultimately, Wills and the Council had looked at ways to make tennis day trippers stay longer, which clearly would increase the economic impact and contribute to the tourism multiplier.

The tournament typically ran from a Saturday to the following Saturday. Qualifying or lesser ranked players started on the first two days. Entrance to the tournament was cheaper in the first few days and became more expensive as the play moved from opening rounds to the later final rounds. On any day visitors could walk around the grounds starting about 10 am, see players practise, attempt to get autographs or pictures, and eat food and drink at some hospitality stands. Further, there were vendors selling tennis equipment and sports clothes. Tournament play usually started at 11 am each day, with matches normally ending about 5–6 pm, although some doubles matches could go longer into the evening, lasting until about 7–8 pm. The tournament took place in June, so there was ample daylight until about 9 pm. Weather was notoriously changeable, with some warm and sunny days, mixed with other times when there was a chance of wind, rain, and some cooler temperatures.

The Council agreed they needed some advice and suggestions on how to make their day tripper tennis fans stay longer and ultimately spend more money in Eastbourne. Wills, as Head of Tourism and Leisure, sought advice now the 2022 version of the tournament had ended in June. She needed to plan well ahead to implement any viable strategies for future editions of the event. She was looking for suggestions that would be financially feasible for the Council to employ, bearing in mind the limited budget the Council had for marketing and for running or supporting events. Her department had a maximum budget of £10,000 that could be allocated to implement any strategies. She would need to think about the cost of implementing any strategy so that the Council would make a solid return on investment in terms of making day trip tennis visitors stay longer.

**Discussion Questions**

1. What are Eastbourne's assets as a destination?
2. How would your group undertake some research to support any advice and suggestions to present to the Council to increase the spend from day tripper tennis fans?
3. Who would your group consult on your strategy and how?
4. What stakeholders need to be considered when undertaking primary research?
5. Does your group have any "out of the box" ideas for the Council to encourage day tripper tennis fans to stay longer and spend more money in Eastbourne?

**Learning Activity: Tourism as an Economic Multiplier**

Read one or more of the journal articles listed in 'References and Suggested Reading' to further understand the types of economic impacts tourists create when visiting a destination. The recommended readings discuss how the tourism multiplier can be strengthened or weakened. Develop a response to the following questions.

1 Identify how the initial tourist expenditure flows through a destination and what business sectors benefit.
2 Read the paper by Wood and Meng (2021) on the Winter Olympics, and identify the economic impacts and direct and indirect links for a sport tourism event.
3 Think about a town or city near you that benefits from the economic impact of tourism, and identify some of the businesses or sectors that indirectly benefit from the tourism multiplier effect.

## Notes

1 World Travel and Tourism Council (2022). *Economic impact reports: United Kingdom.* (online) Available at: https://wttc.org/DesktopModules/MVC/FactSheets/pdf/704/228_20220613171619_UnitedKingdom2022_.pdf
2 Geertsma, M. (2022). The challenges and opportunities of retaining customers in a changed travel & meetings environment. *Hospitality Net.* (online) Available at: https://www.hospitalitynet.org/news/4112298.html
3 Deloitte (2013). *Tourism jobs and growth: The economic contribution of the tourism economy in the UK.* (online) Available at: https://www.visitbritain.org/sites/default/files/vb-corporate/Documents-Library/documents/Tourism_Jobs_and_Growth_2013.pdf

## References and Suggested Reading

Deloitte (2013). *Tourism jobs and growth: The economic contribution of the tourism economy in the UK.* (online) Available at: https://www.visitbritain.org/sites/default/files/vbcorporate/Documents-Library/documents/Tourism_Jobs_and_Growth_2013.pdf

Geertsma, M. (2022). The challenges and opportunities of retaining customers in a changed travel & meetings environment. *Hospitality Net.* (online) Available at: https://www.hospitalitynet.org/news/4112298.html

World Travel and Tourism Council (2022). *Economic impact reports: United Kingdom.* (online) Available at: https://wttc.org/DesktopModules/MVC/FactSheets/pdf/704/228_20220613171619_UnitedKingdom2022_.pdf

## Recommended Readings

Fretchling, D. C., & Horváth, E. (1999). Estimating the multiplier effects of tourism expenditures on a local economy through a regional input-output model. *Journal of Travel Research, 37*, 324–332.

Robles Teigeiro, L., & Díaz, B. (2014). Estimation of multipliers for the activity of hotels and restaurants. *Tourism Management, 40*, 27–34.

Wall, G. (1997). Scale effects on tourism multipliers. *Annals of Tourism Research, 24*(2), 447–450.

Wood, J., & Meng, S. (2021). The economic impacts of the 2018 Winter Olympics. *Tourism Economics, 27*(7), 1303–1322.

## Exhibits

### **Exhibit 13.1** Location of Eastbourne Tennis Tournament

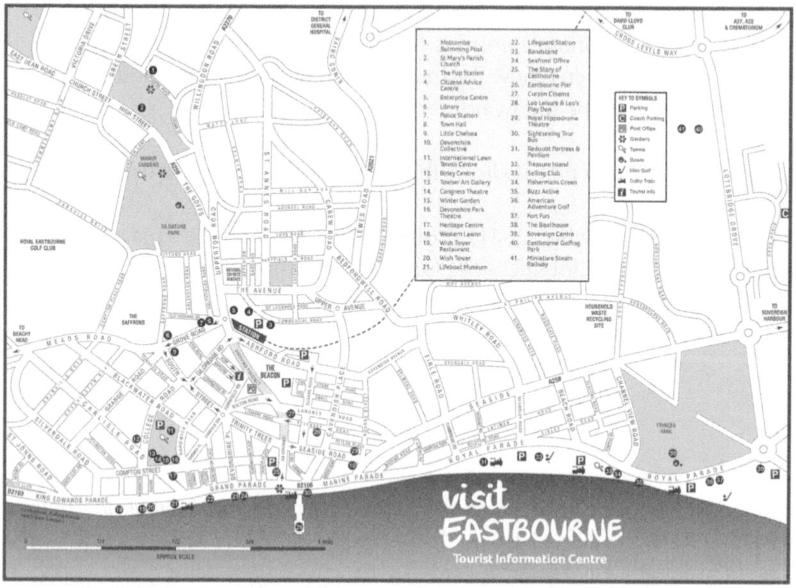


Source: With permission from Eastbourne County Council.

### **Exhibit 13.2** Women's Doubles International Eastbourne Tennis Tournament Serena Williams (foreground) Returns to Play with Ons Jabeur, Centre Court, June 2022

Source: Photo courtesy of Nigel Jarvis (author).

**Exhibit 13.3** Women's Final, International Eastbourne Tennis Tournament Petra Kvitová versus Jelena Ostapenko, Centre Court, June 2022

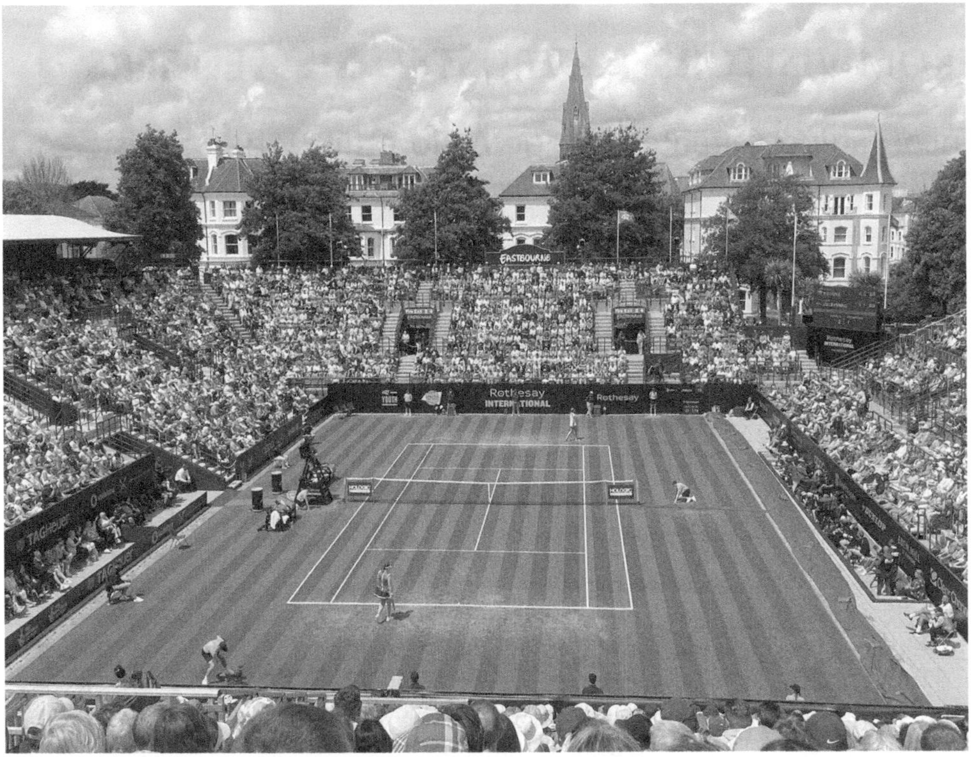


Source: Photo courtesy of Nigel Jarvis (author).

# CASE 14

## FROM VISITORS TO TRUSTED MESSENGERS

### Encouraging Climate Change Action through Post-visit Action Resources

*Christine Van Winkle and Jill Bueddefeld*

**Synopsis**

The Assiniboine Park Zoo (APZ), operated by the not-for-profit Assiniboine Park Conservancy, had a strong conservation and research mandate that focused on arctic and subarctic species. This case explores how, after an on-site experience, attractions can connect with visitors beyond the initial visit, to build lasting relationships and develop "trusted messengers" who would later contribute to the organization's mandate and conservation action. While the sustainability and conservation messages at the centre of the zoo's mandate were clear throughout the exhibits, there remained an opportunity to connect the on-site experience with the visitors' potential agency in conservation and sustainability once they left the attraction.

The Assiniboine Park Zoo (APZ)[1], located on 80 acres within the City of Winnipeg, was a featured attraction within Winnipeg and the Province of Manitoba, Canada (Exhibit 14.1). The year-round attraction had both indoor and outdoor exhibits with more that 150 species from around the world. In April 2017, Stephen Petersen, Head of Conservation and Research at APZ, returned to thinking about one of his key goals, which was to inspire visitors to value wild things and wild places by educating them through, and about, conservation action. Petersen believed it essential to work with the passionate and knowledgeable zoo team to explore how to encourage visitors to become "trusted messengers." A "trusted messenger" would be a visitor who, at the end of their experience at the zoo, was prepared with high-quality knowledge to share a message about conservation and climate change action.

As a conservation and research institute, the APZ was committed to ensuring exhibits did more than entertain. The flagship exhibit "The Journey to Churchill" was designed with interpretive, emotional, and behavioural objectives to facilitate learning and connection with the arctic (Exhibit 14.2). This was in line with the United Nations Sustainable Development

DOI: 10.4324/9781003280040-20

goal 13 – Take Urgent Action to Combat Climate Change and Its Impacts[2]. Petersen was optimistic about what could be accomplished and was determined to work collaboratively to encourage zoo visitors to take pro-environmental action. The SDG was urgent, and the APZ's response had the same urgency.

## The Assiniboine Park Zoo

The Assiniboine Park Zoo had been a beloved attraction in Winnipeg, Canada, since 1959 (Exhibit 14.3). The first major redevelopment of the zoo began in 2000, and resulted in improvements to infrastructure, animal enclosures and educational spaces. As an accredited member of the Association of Zoos and Aquariums, Canada's Accredited Zoos and Aquariums, and the World Association of Zoos and Aquariums, the APZ was committed to the highest standard of animal care and was dedicated to research, conservation, and education. Educational programs were developed for diverse ages and visitor groups.

## The Journey to Churchill

Opened in 2014, The Journey to Churchill (JTC) experience at the APZ was an award-winning exhibit and a featured destination in the city and province. The ten-acre exhibit showcased arctic and subarctic habitats and wildlife, including muskox, caribou, arctic foxes, wolves, snowy owls, seals, and polar bears[3] The interpretive centre gave visitors insight into the important role that researchers and conservation staff played in protecting abandoned polar bear cubs from Churchill, Manitoba. At the zoo, the cubs were cared for, and when they had a clean bill of health and could safely interact with the other, larger polar bears, they joined the larger polar bear enclosure. The "barrier-free" exhibit provided an illusion of being in a landscape with rock walls and wall-size windows and tunnels, so visitors had views of multiple animals simultaneously (Exhibit 14.4). Whether through floor-to-ceiling windows, outdoor exhibits, underwater tunnels, or while eating lunch in the cafeteria, visitors had remarkable close-up views of the bears, and were captivated by their image and behaviour. Besides viewing bears and other animals, visitors could learn about arctic flora and fauna through keeper talks, volunteer docents, a film in the 360-degree theatre, and through interpretive displays that stood throughout the site. While the interpretive elements and animals were the heart and soul of the exhibit, there were opportunities for visitors to play together at the indoor polar theme playground, on the decommissioned helicopter and snowmobiles along the pathways, and at a small outdoor climbing structure shaped like a whale skeleton (Exhibit 14.5).

The Journey to Churchill exhibit was described to visitors as a place to:

> Experience a variety of naturalistic landscapes and animal viewing areas. Interpretive signage and interactive displays invite visitors to learn about biodiversity, climate change and conservation. It is an educational classroom like no other, inviting exploration, challenging thinking, and promoting personal action.
>
> (Assiniboine Park Conservancy, 2017)

The exhibit was thoughtfully designed to engage emotionally and physically by situating visitors within a space with plenty of opportunity to learn, play, and experience elements of life in a replicated arctic town.

### The Purpose of the Exhibits – More than Entertainment

Petersen, the Head of Conservation and Research, wanted to work across zoo departments (education, marketing, volunteer management) to ensure the visitors left the zoo with a connection to the arctic that would contribute to the zoo's climate change objectives and, more broadly to the UN SDGs. Specifically, all staff hoped zoo visitors would leave with increased knowledge about the arctic and subarctic region and species, emotionally engage and connect with the animals, and ultimately change their behaviours to reflect support for conservation and research. Past research showed that thoughtfully designed interpretive experiences could affect sustainability knowledge, attitudes, and behaviours[4]. Peterson believed that wildlife tourism experiences that shared messages about climate change and sustainability were important for conservation and promoting environmental sustainability. However, the team at APZ had limited understanding of how these experiences could directly lead to sustainability. The UN SDG 13 stated that "Through education, innovation and adherence to our climate commitments, we can make the necessary changes to protect the planet."[2]

### Research for Change

The staff agreed it was important to connect visitors' learning at the zoo to climate action. Petersen and the zoo team wanted to understand how the Journey to Churchill exhibit could encourage visitors to consider sustainability and climate change mitigation in their own lives. To better understand the visitors' experiences, two separate studies were undertaken in collaboration with university researchers.

The first study explored the use of post-visit action resources (PVARs)[5]. PVARs were resources visitors could use after their on-site experience to extend the learning experience. Common forms of PVARs were printed handouts, email updates, and, more recently, social media engagement. The results of a mixed-method study to explore the use of PVARs after a visit to the JTC showed conflicting results. Participants who received PVARs felt that their behaviour had changed. Yet, in the survey data there were no significant differences in sustainable behaviour found between these visitors and visitors who received material unrelated to the key messages at the site. The qualitative follow-up interviews indicated that *some* visitors had made significant behavioural changes. These changes were outside those suggested in the survey scale (Exhibit 14.6). These findings indicated that the messaging could impact visitors, just not all visitors, and not in the ways anticipated.

The second study sought to understand the on-site learning experience at the JTC. The researchers found that personal, sociocultural, and physical onsite experiences resulted in learning experiences that involved communicating, reflecting, and personal transformation. While it was clear that learning occurred during the visit, it remained uncertain how this learning would change visitors' day-to-day lives regarding sustainability and climate change.

The studies suggested that changing people's behaviour was challenging but that people were meaningfully impacted by their experiences at the JTC and appeared to want to do more to reduce their negative impact on the environment. After learning about the studies' findings, Petersen worked collaboratively with the Zoo's Head of Education to reflect on how best to enhance the visitor experience on-site to further facilitate learning experiences that would be simultaneously entertaining, educational, memorable, inspiring, and implementable. One area that Petersen wanted to explore further was how to encourage visitors to become "trusted messengers."

## Trusted Messengers

"Trusted messenger" was a concept from health care and climate change that researchers found could be relevant to the APZs vision to engage visitors after they left the site. Trusted messengers were traditionally either 1) experts who could communicate well with the public or 2) community leaders with special training to communicate with the public about complex topics[6] However, research had shown that individuals who were not experts, but rather knowledgeable and passionate members of the public, could effectively communicate important issues through their own narratives[7]. People could offer powerful personal insight into learning and behaviour change. Petersen was convinced that through a combination of on-site programming, communication, and marketing, the APZ could build lasting relationships with visitors and motivate visitors to change their behaviour to combat climate change and related impacts.

As part of the zoo team, Petersen was inspired to work with the team to identify approaches and practices to encourage visitors to become "trusted messengers" who would leave the APZ and share well-informed climate action messages. The team hoped to have initiatives in place within six months so that he and the team could monitor the impact and their contribution to SDG Goal 13.

### Discussion Questions

1 What were the different ways that the APZ facilitated visitor on-site experiences that contributed to climate action to protect the planet?
2 How can zoo staff encourage/educate visitors to be trusted messengers for climate action after their initial zoo visit?
3 How should Petersen and the team monitor or evaluate the impact of their actions and visitor programs over the next six months?

### Learning Activity

Review the United Nations Sustainable Development Goal 13 online at https://sdgs.un.org/goals/goal13.

Take a virtual tour of the Journey to Churchill exhibit https://www.youtube.com/watch?v=DyjHgEHjazw and review the Assiniboine Park Zoo (APZ) website https://www.assiniboinepark.ca/zoo/animals/journey-to-churchill.

Read one of the following studies on post-visit action resources (PVAR).

Bueddefeld, J. N., & Van Winkle, C. M. (2017). Exploring the effect of zoo post-visit action resources on sustainable behavior change. *Journal of Sustainable Tourism, 25*(9), 1205–1221.

Hughes, K. (2011). Designing post-visit action resources for families visiting wildlife tourism sites. *Visitor Studies, 14*(1), 66–83.

Now you understand the role of PVAR in visitor learning, develop a post-visit action resource that is informed by a visit to the JTC and that that allows visitors to address SDG 13 after their on-site visit. Conduct an online search to explore various formats for PVAR used by other, related institutions (zoos, museums, aquariums, interpretive centres). Then, select a format for your PVAR (on-line, paper based, email, or others). Next consider the topic for the PVAR (climate change, global warming, wildlife habitat loss or other). Finally, create an activity for visitors to do that is described within the PVAR and relates to SDG 13. Consider sharing and reviewing your work with other students to see the different ideas and approaches taken.

## Notes

1 Assiniboine Park Zoo website, https://www.assiniboinepark.ca/zoo/visit/hours-and-rates
2 United Nations Sustainable Development Goals, https://sdgs.un.org/goals/goal13
3 https://www.assiniboinepark.ca/zoo/animals/journey-to-churchill
4 Van Winkle, C. M., & Bueddefeld, J. N. (2016). Service-dominant logic and the festival experience. *International Journal of Event and Festival Management*
5 Bueddefeld, J. N., & Van Winkle, C. M. (2017). Exploring the effect of zoo post-visit action resources on sustainable behavior change. *Journal of Sustainable Tourism*, *25*(9), 1205–1221. Hughes, K. (2011). Designing post-visit action resources for families visiting wildlife tourism sites. *Visitor Studies*, *14*(1), 66–83.
6 Howarth, C., Parsons, L., & Thew, H. (2020). Effectively communicating climate science beyond academia: Harnessing the heterogeneity of climate knowledge. *One Earth*, *2*(4), 320–324.
7 Moser, S. C. (2010). Communicating climate change: history, challenges, process and future directions. *Wiley Interdisciplinary Reviews: Climate Change*, *1*(1), 31–53.

## References and Suggested Reading

Bueddefeld, J. N., & Van Winkle, C. M. (2017). Exploring the effect of zoo post-visit action resources on sustainable behavior change. *Journal of Sustainable Tourism*, *25*(9), 1205–1221.

Howarth, C., Parsons, L., & Thew, H. (2020). Effectively communicating climate science beyond academia: Harnessing the heterogeneity of climate knowledge. *One Earth*, *2*(4), 320–324

Hughes, K. (2011). Designing post-visit action resources for families visiting wildlife tourism sites. *Visitor Studies*, *14*(1), 66–83.

Moser, S. C. (2010). Communicating climate change: History, challenges, process and future directions. *Wiley Interdisciplinary Reviews: Climate Change*, *1*(1), 31–53

Van Winkle, C. M., & Bueddefeld, J. N. (2016). Service-dominant logic and the festival experience. *International Journal of Event and Festival Management*, *7*(3), 237–254.

## Exhibits

### Exhibit 14.1 Map of North America with Location of Winnipeg, Manitoba, Canada

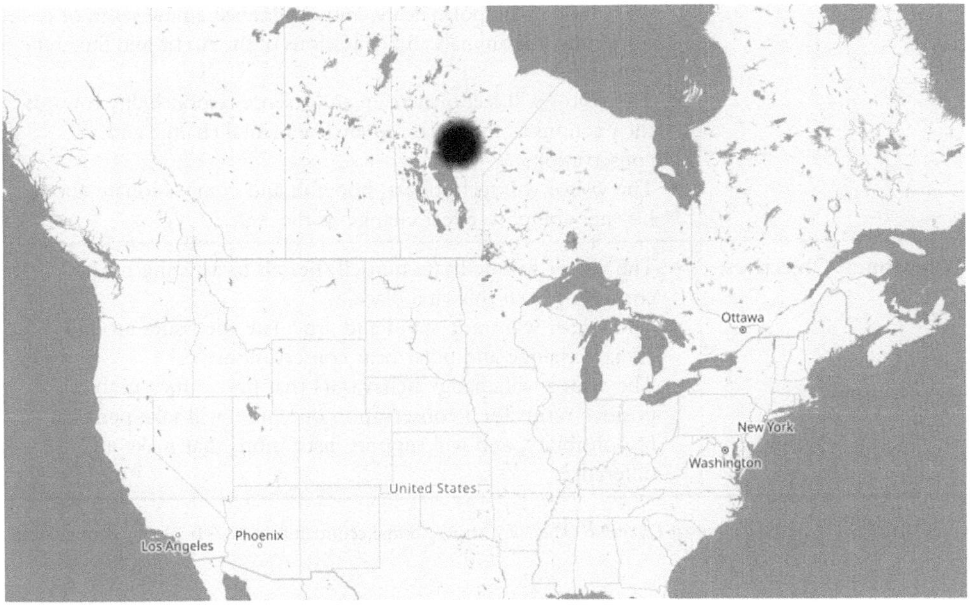


Source: OpenStreetMap. Data available under open database License. For more information see openstreetmap.org/copyright.

### Exhibit 14.2 APZ Journey to Churchill Objectives

| Objectives | Descriptions |
|---|---|
| **Interpretive Objectives** | • The visitor will learn the basic ingredients for life in the extreme conditions of the Arctic's vast, beautiful expanse, including how animals and people are adapted to seasons, day/night cycles, isolation, extreme winds, and subzero temperatures.<br>• The visitor will connect through emotions and science to a complete picture of the effects of environmental change on the Arctic, especially on polar bears, and understand their role in, and effect on, the ecosystem.<br>• The visitor will engage with the body of science re: Arctic and climate change, discover global efforts on polar bear conservation and institutional transparency, and gain an understanding of what support is needed.<br>• The visitor will be motivated to learn more about the Arctic and Subarctic, and to visit Churchill and Wapusk National Park.<br>• The visitors will learn about research that is being done with and by Zoo partners. |

*(Continued)*

**Exhibit 14.2** (Continued)

| | |
|---|---|
| **Emotional Objectives:** | • The visitor will experience a soaring sense of joy at the beauty of the polar bears and their environment depicted in the exhibits, feel pride toward the Zoo and Manitoba for the work being done on behalf of the polar bears, and experience a new sense of respect for the animals and conditions of the Arctic and Subarctic regions.<br>• The visitor will feel ownership and a sense responsibility towards their actions as they relate to environmental change and conservation.<br>• The visitor will feel upbeat, hopeful, and compassionate about his/her ability to affect change in the Arctic. |
| **Behavioural Objectives:** | • The visitor will dedicate himself/herself to assisting in the conservation of this vital place.<br>• The visitor will understand and articulate the issues around climate change and polar bear conservation.<br>• The visitor will change behaviours that have a measurable, positive result for a conservation outcome, will take personal responsibility, and will support institutions that make a difference. |

Source: Benbow, M (n.d.). *Journey to Churchill Objectives.* http://home.cc.umanitoba.ca/~benbow/zootalk.html.

**Exhibit 14.3** Children Playing at the Assiniboine Park Zoo in the 1960s

Source: Archives Manitoba, government photographs, 1960. (Assiniboine Park Zoo).

**Exhibit 14.4** View of Polar Bear Swimming from JTC Viewing Tunnel

Source: Photo courtesy of Jill Bueddefeld (author).

**Exhibit 14.5** Outdoor Trails in the Journey to Churchill Exhibit

Source: Photo courtesy of Jill Bueddefeld (author).

**Exhibit 14.6** Changes in Behaviour after Zoo Visit Described by Visitors

| Increased Behaviours | New Behaviours |
|---|---|
| "Reducing the amount of water used for showers, laundry, dishes, etc. around the house" | "Encouraging my kids to be aware of sustainability" |
| "I actually found I turn the lights/electronics off when I leave the room now. Used to be more diligent about it but was slacking off. The exhibit was a nice reminder I should do it always not just sometimes". | "Conscious of turning off lights, and not letting water flow as long. Looking to use less plastic, and reuse items when able to" |
| "Buying locally grown food. Planting a vegetable garden" (Participant 348); "Composting more, ensuring shutting off electronics when not being used" | "Being more conscious of my carbon footprint, trying to buy local where possible" |
| "Have increased emphasis on recycling as well as avoidance of pesticides and herbicides" | "I have started to recycle myself since I have my own house. Starting to prepare my garden for next year" |
| "We began composting" | "Bought a rain barrel" |
| "Turning off lights and electronics more. Farmer's market shopping for local food" | "I'm going to try and buy more locally produced food. I might volunteer as well in the future" |

Source: Bueddefeld, J. N., & Van Winkle, C. M. (2017). Exploring the effect of zoo post-visit action resources on sustainable behavior change. *Journal of Sustainable Tourism*, *25*(9), 1205–1221.

# CASE 15

## THE LOCAL WILD FOOD CHALLENGE

### Translating a Chef's Passion for Wild Food into a Sustainable Event

*Ingrid Kajzer Mitchell, Rebecca Wilson-Mah, and Christine Van Winkle*

**Synopsis**

Chef Bill Manson created a small community event, the "Local Wild Food Challenge," in 2008 in Eastbourne, New Zealand. By 2018, the event had become a network of communities holding yearly events in different countries celebrating the culinary skills of local people. With expansion, Manson recognised that he needed to give more consideration to community event planning and organisation while also staying true to his commitment to inclusivity and promoting sustainability of local resources.

On October 20, 2018, the day before the Local Wild Food Challenge (LWFC), Chef Bill Manson headed out to the Farm Institute at the eastern end of Martha's Vineyard, an island south of Cape Cod, on the northeast coast of the United States. The Farm Institute at the Katama farm, dedicated to sustainable agriculture and farm education, was once again the location for the culinary adventure competition Manson founded ten years earlier. The LWFC was a unique event with only one requirement – the competing dishes had to include at least one wild ingredient.

As Manson passed the little harbour towns and farmland, he admired the beautiful fall views of the island that had now become his second home. In the October off-season, the island was less busy now, the bustling summer days and big tourist crowds long gone. As Manson reached the farm he watched as a group of volunteers slowly transformed the grass field in front of him into an event venue. Over the years, Manson had seen participation grow from 50 visitors to 500. Still, he wondered, would enough competing participants register, and would visitors show up for the competitions? Would they feel included in the wild food community he had helped to build? Would it inspire them to see the real opportunities of wild foods, like he did?

DOI: 10.4324/9781003280040-21

### Local Wild Food Challenge

The LWFC began as a small community event in 2008 in Eastbourne, New Zealand. It had come a long way since the early days and had grown to become a global network of communities holding yearly events in four different countries: Finland, New Zealand, Italy, and the United States. Manson's original idea was to get foragers, hunters, and fishers together for a friendly and relaxed contest to celebrate the knowledge of the land, and the skills and talents of local people. He had a vision to recognise and applaud local culinary talent.

In 2008, Manson had not known the first event would be the start a series of festivals with a focus on local wild food. Nine years on since the first LWFC, the goal was still to celebrate community and, at the same time, generate awareness of natural resources and the local environment. The LWFC's mission posted on its website, was to "promote understanding, appreciation and sustainability" of local resources grounded in the belief that "the deeper you venture into your environment the more motivation you have to protect it" (http://www.localwildfoodchallenge.com/about/).

The LWFC was fun and accessible, with registration inclusive and free of charge. Everyone was invited to participate – from home cooks to professional chefs – regardless of age and skill level. Previous LWFC events had attracted between 25 and 65 competing professional and home cook chefs. Through their active participation in the event the competing participants played a leading role in facilitating the experience, simultaneously being both producers (e.g., preparing the food themselves, exchanging knowledge with visitors) and consumers of the event (e.g., learning new food preparation techniques skills) (Exhibit 15.1). Moreover, Manson encouraged what he referred to as "multi-generational awareness," where young and old could get out into their local natural environment to source wild ingredients through hunting, fishing, foraging, bartering, or gathering, and learn about natural ingredients not commonly found in commercial stores. While children had not initially been a target audience in the early days, they had now become an integral part of the LWFC. Many of them returned as young adults and entered the competition on their own. In 2013, the LWFC at Martha's Vineyard introduced a competition category for children to enter and participate.

In 2018, the LWFC community was known for its camaraderie and community ethos. Manson saw himself as a convener of a community, rather than a formal event organiser. Some participants travelled across the world to volunteer and compete. LWFC was also known for its strong educational focus. As Manson saw it, wild food education had an essential role, and this was very much at the heart of every food challenge, in any event location. Over the last decade, Manson had sought to educate participants around "what is available, what is possible" with wild foods. At LWFC visitors were encouraged to interact with participating chefs, and there was always a wide range of educational demo sessions and workshops (Exhibit 15.2). For example, there were fish filleting demonstrations (how to not waste your catch, how to fillet the fish), artisans demonstrating traditional cooking techniques, or the use of uncommon ingredients (e.g., racoon meat, worms), and "hunter-to-punter" demonstrations (e.g., showing the natural chain of deer meat in front of spectators). Manson hoped that participants would realise that wild foods, often ignored or thrown away, had the potential to be a decent, healthy, and viable food source.

## About Bill Manson and the Founding Family

Manson, a New Zealander, had spent the last ten years dividing his time between Martha's Vineyard (MV) and his native home in Eastbourne, New Zealand. The outdoors had always been important to Manson, and throughout his career as a chef he had sought out opportunities to combine his two passions, food and nature. An avid surfer, he had many friends who also enjoyed hunting, fishing, and gathering wild foods. The idea of the LWFC came to him after he and his wife had lived and worked in the French Alps running an adventure tourism and food venture. Learning about the local, and regional, foods and the lengths to which the locals would go to source and forage natural ingredients, inspired Manson. The effort, physicality, and interaction it took to find and source food ingredients were very rewarding to him. Upon return to Eastbourne, the idea of a local food competition started to take off.

Manson took great pride in the wild food community he had helped to create. He enjoyed the relationships with local community groups, volunteers, competing participants and visitors. To him, everyone played a lead role to co-create this unique gastronomic experience. Manson believed that when competing participants prepared and assembled the dishes on the day of the event, other participants, volunteers, and visitors had the opportunity to learn something new and had access to the wild food expertise and knowledge of locals. It was important to Manson that the LWFC was user-friendly and that visitors were empowered to try wild food foraging and cooking themselves. Manson also felt a personal responsibility to help educate attendees about respecting and protecting natural local resources. For him, both the protection and use of wild foods went "hand in hand," and allowed himself and others to "get back and keep using wild resources while having generations beyond use it as well."

With his wife Sarah, Manson had overseen many of the LWFC event responsibilities such as administration, design, and operations (volunteer coordination, the venue, and sponsorship agreements). They operated LWFC events using their own finances and relied on their own personal networks. Manson's longtime friend and fellow wild food enthusiast Jim Thompson helped with marketing and publicity and created video content of the events. Each LWFC yielded a small profit that was put back into support for the next event. In the last few years, as the demand for the event had grown, Manson had tried to step back from the event set up and sponsorship work. He actively worked to hand over some of the event planning responsibilities to local partners and community members to ensure the long-term future viability of the LWFC.

## The Martha's Vineyard Event

The event followed a typical LWFC format. Like other LWFC events it was held in a rural location, away from suburbs and busy city centres. Registration for the event was through the LWFC website or on the day of the event with an entry form provided at the venue. The event started at 11 am and continued to 6 pm, with food entries judged between 12 pm and 3 pm. The event had a casual program that included concurrent live interactive wild food demonstrations, food sampling tables, workshops, food trucks, a bar with beer and wine, and live music (Exhibit 15.3). The competition was intentionally "open to everyone," including chefs from local restaurants, caterers, home cooks, hunter-gatherers, fishers, and children (Exhibit 15.4). All dishes entered had to be pre-prepared, and there were prep-tables and equipment such as ovens and grills to finish off the dishes. Once dishes were ready, they were taken to the judging table for scoring.

A panel of judges tasted and scored the dishes based on four categories. In addition to local ingredients, taste and presentation, points were assigned for the degree of effort the contestant had given to sourcing the wild ingredients and to dish preparation. The judging and scoring system were therefore intentionally designed to create a level playing field for home cooks and professional chefs. Competing participants were encouraged to write a 100–200 word story that detailed how they had gathered and prepared their dishes. This gave the judges insight into the sourcing of the ingredients and the challenges the participants might have faced. Everyone was encouraged to have fun, and to connect with each other across their community to source a wide variety of wild and local ingredients. After dishes were judged, they were taken to the tasting table for visitors to try.

Volunteer activities at the event included helping at the registration table, showing competing participants the cooking facilities, taking ready dishes to the judges, and managing the tasting table. All volunteers were given a black LWFC t-shirt or shirt to wear. The prize categories included a grand prize, runner up, and a third place, but also awarded categories such as best effort, wildest ingredient, best water, best forest and land, best use of local ingredients, best dessert, children's grand prize, children's runner up, and children's best effort. Each prize category was accompanied with a gift from one of the many local sponsors.

Promotion of the event included the LWFC website, posters, and flyers in highly visited local areas, social media posts on the LWFC Facebook page and Instagram account, sponsorship agreements, and local media exposure prior to and after the event (Exhibit 15.3). The LWFC also relied heavily on word-of-mouth. Post-event activities included posting photos or video material, and sharing specific updates on the winners on social media channels. LWFC also had a YouTube channel to share short videos related to the event (Exhibit 15.4).

### Attendees' Motivations and Experiences

The LWFC attracted a broad range of attendees, either entering to compete or spectating. Attendees included professional chefs, home cooks, foragers, hunter-gatherers, fishers, restauranteurs, locals, tourists, and children. Manson always tried to ensure that as many people were represented and celebrated as possible. In 2017, to find out more about visitors, Manson partnered with researchers from a Canadian university. The researchers interviewed 24 visitors and six competing participants at Martha's Vineyard and found that visitors had prior knowledge, experience of, and interest in wild foods and 50% of the interviewed visitors had attended one or more LWFC events. Some foraged occasionally, and others had more extensive experience. The main reason for attending the event was their personal connection to Manson or to a volunteer. Other reasons included trying new and different kinds of food, learning about wild foods, supporting the local community, and a general interest in local foods. Some visitors were less attracted to the wild food focus and were mainly motivated by the idea of "getting outside" and having "something fun to do." Many of the competing participants had continued to forage and prepare wild foods throughout the year for their own consumption. Attendees' motivations for gathering, preparing, and consuming wild foods included self-sufficiency, a desire to know their food source, perceived health and environmental benefits, and the personal satisfaction and empowerment of "cooking something you have caught yourself." A few also expressed motivation to be less reliant on mass-produced foods and mainstream food systems.

Overall, attendees were very satisfied with their experience, and many remarked on the commitment of the organisers, the friendly atmosphere, and the community building that took place. However, attendees noted it was not an event to simply attend for an hour or so. It was necessary to stay for the duration of the event to experience it fully. For example, sampling of dishes did not start until later in the day, and if visitors came early or left early, they missed some of the key attractions. Visitors and competing participants who had previously attended a LWFC shared how their awareness of local wild food had increased with each attendance. Return attendees also shared that they appreciated learning about the local community and the skills of local people. First-time attendees noted the experience had opened their eyes to different kinds of food, and to the accessibility of wild foods.

## Next Steps for the Local Wild Food Challenge

As Manson parked his car at the Farm Institute and stepped out to help the volunteers finalise the set up for the next day, he was reminded of his long-standing ambition for a global movement of LWFC events. He lived and breathed this dream. With continued growth he knew he needed to revisit his current event planning approach to ensure events like this one at Martha's Vineyard were financially sustainable as they matured and that attendees continued to have a positive experience. In the research carried out by the Canadian university, attendees had commented that it would be helpful to have more event advertising, a more detailed schedule indicating when activities were taking place, improved wayfinding on site, better signage for the prepared dishes, and more activities and educational content overall both prior, during, and after the event. Next year, in 2019, the event was to return to Martha's Vineyard and once again was tentatively scheduled for the end of October. Manson vowed to make some changes in the event planning process and the organisation of the educational content of the event, while staying close to his values around sustainability and inclusivity.

### Discussion Questions

1 What strengths and potential gaps can you identify in the event management process at the LWFC?
2 Thinking about co-creation and inclusivity, what do you consider to be the essential elements of the event experience at the LWFC in Martha's Vineyard? What new opportunities might you identify?
3 In your view is this event sustainable? What kind of pro-environmental behaviours can be encouraged in this setting?
4 How could Bill build and sustain attendee engagement before, during, and after the LWFC event?

### Learning Activity: A Focus on an Experiential Model and Co-creation in Gastronomic Tourism Experiences

Richards, G. (2015). Evolving gastronomic experiences: From food to foodies to foodscapes. *Journal of Gastronomy and Tourism, 1,* 1–14.

Read this article about the development of the relationship between gastronomy and tourism.

In the article Richards (2015) identifies three generations of change that are named as stages in the development of the relationship between gastronomy and tourism. The stages are as follows:

*First Generation:* The production of themed experiences for consumers
*Second Generation:* The co-creation of experiences by producers and consumers
*Third Generation:* The development of communities around gastronomy and food

Consider the following questions:

1 How are first, second, and third generation represented in the LWFC?
2 Consider first generation and the production of themed experiences for consumers, and answer the following:
    - Is the LWFC themed? What would you consider to be the content of the theme?
    - In what ways do experiences at LWFC stimulate the attendee/consumer?
    - What more could be done to establish first-generation connections between gastronomy and tourism?
3 Consider second generation and the co-creation of experiences by producers and consumers, and answer the following:
    - What co-creation opportunities are offered at the LWFC event?
    - What new opportunities for co-creation experiences are possible when launching the event in a new location?
    - What more could be done to establish second-generation connections between gastronomy and tourism?
4 Consider the third generation and the development of communities around gastronomy and food, and answer the following:
    - In what ways does the LWFC community create an opportunity for connections to be made between food and place, identity, culture, and tourism?
    - In what ways is the LWFC community inclusive and/or participatory? Explain your response.
    - What more could be done to establish third-generation connections between gastronomy and tourism?

## References and Suggested Reading

Bueddefeld, J., & Van Winkle, C. (2018). The role of post-visit action resources in facilitating meaningful free-choice learning after a zoo visit. *Environmental Education Research, 24*(1), 97–110.

Collins, A., & Cooper, C. (2017). Measuring and managing the environmental impact of festivals: The contribution of the ecological footprint. *Journal of Sustainable Tourism*, *25*(1), 148–162.
de Brito, M. P., & Terzieva, L. (2016). Key elements for designing a strategy to generate social and environmental value: A comparative study of festivals. *Research in Hospitality Management*, *6*(1), 51–59.
Laing, J., & Frost, W. (2010). How green was my festival: Exploring challenges and opportunities associated with staging green events. *International Journal of Hospitality Management*, *29*(2), 261–267.
Prebensen, N. K., & Foss, L. (2010). Coping and co-creating in tourist experiences. *International Journal of Tourism Research*, *13*(1), 54–67.
Richards, G. (2015). Evolving gastronomic experiences: From food to foodies to foodscapes. *Journal of Gastronomy and Tourism*, *1*, 1–14.
Silvers, J. R., Bowdin, G. A., O'Toole, W. J., & Nelson, K. B. (2005). Towards an international event management body of knowledge (EMBOK). *Event Management*, *9*(4), 185–198.
Van Winkle, C., & Bueddefeld, J. (2020). Free-choice learning in agritourism. *World Leisure Journal*, *63*(2), 182–200.

## Exhibits

### Exhibit 15.1 Demonstrations

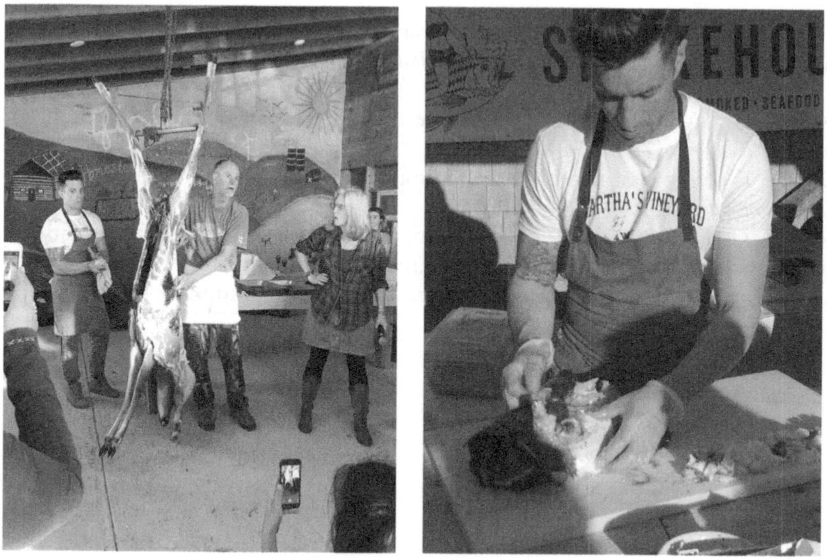

Source: Author's own and with permission from the LWFC.

### Exhibit 15.2 Program and Food Sampling, and Interactive Activities (e.g., Making Apple Juice)

Source: Author's own and with permission from the LWFC.

**Exhibit 15.3** Post-event News Article 2017, LWFC, Martha's Vineyard

https://www.mvtimes.com/2017/10/23/care-little-bbq-racoon/?fbclid=IwAR3ppKDayIFp_nGqOj5VvAH8bVXPs3eu7z-IkH7DHvJ_giBA1bovBdVeP7c

**Exhibit 15.4** Videos Posted on YouTube Channel

Local Wild Food Challenge Taster https://www.youtube.com/watch?v=1zl3MfckC6Q

Local Wild Food Challenge Martha's Vineyard 2016 – The winners https://www.youtube.com/watch?v=7brp9hGD8Qg

# INDEX

Note: Page numbers in **bold** indicate exhibits; page numbers in italics tables; and page numbers followed by "n" indicate notes.